— Praise for *Building Behavioral Science in an Organization* —

"Many organizations want to leverage behavioral science but struggle to turn insight into impact. This book is an excellent guide for practitioners seeking to build their behavioral science muscle across their organization."

— NIR EYAL, bestselling author of *Hooked* and *Indistractable*

"An invaluable resource for anyone interested in getting into the field of applied behavioral science, or applying its findings and methods more intentionally."

— ALINE HOLZWARTH, Head of Behavioral Science at Pattern Health

"They simplify the complexity and uncertainty of this field in a way that provides comfort, assurance and guidance to individuals and organizations building a behavioral science practice. The authors and their partners address the many opportunities and challenges in turn, while laying out strategies for success that apply to the evolving realities of getting the job done."

— JEFF KREISLER, Managing Director & Head of Behavioral Science at JPMorgan Chase & Co.

"Building Behavioral Science in an Organization is a vital resource for behavioral science practitioners and organizations exploring how to embrace behavioral science. The book is full of case examples, useful anecdotes and discussions of barriers and opportunities for incorporating behavioral science within an organization. The contributing authors are highly sought-after experts in the field and provide excellent guidance that you can bring directly back to your organization."

— CHRISTOPHER NAVE, PhD, Managing Director, Penn Master of Behavioral & Decision Sciences Program

Building Behavioral Science in an Organization

EDITED BY

Zarak Khan & Laurel Newman

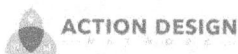

Penn
Master of Behavioral
and Decision Sciences

ACTION DESIGN

Published by Action Design Press
4009 Longfellow Street
Hyattsville, MD 20781
Publisher@Action-Design.org

Book Design by Kory Kirby
SET IN MINION PRO

ISBN 978-1-7366525-0-3 (paperback)
ISBN 978-1-7366525-1-0 (eBook)

Printed in the United States of America

Contents

PART I

INTRODUCTION

Preface

Zarak Khan & Laurel Newman

Behavioral science is an umbrella term that includes social psychology, behavioral economics, sociology, and other academic disciplines. It can be applied to a variety of practice areas within an organization via a range of design and measurement tactics. It can influence strategy and design throughout an organization, including such areas as product design, marketing and communications, employee and customer engagement, and strategic decision making. In practice people often end up specializing in one area or another, but applied behavioral science includes both designing for the moment (the domain of nudges and cognitive biases) as well as creating the broader context for shaping the thoughts, emotions, and behavioral patterns of employees and customers.

As applied behavioral science has become more widespread, a need has emerged for guidance on how to build and integrate behavioral science functions within an organization. This book attempts to provide some guidance by drawing on the collective wisdom of applied behavioral scientists with deep experience within their respective practice areas. It is meant to be a quick start guide for both organization leaders and behavioral scientists on where and how to integrate behavioral science into your organization.

The first two sections highlight the growth of applied behavioral science and key practice areas within an organization where it can be employed. Ideally this provides some guidance to organization leaders, for instance a VP of Marketing or Chief Innovation Officer, on why behavioral science is useful and how to integrate it into their respective area. The final section details key considerations in setting up and growing a behavioral science function, and would be useful to both organizational champions and the behavioral science leaders tasked with implementation.

We're providing the digital version of this book for free. As part of the non-profit Action Design Network, Action Design Press shares the mission of making behavioral science more accessible to people. Founded in 2012, Action Design Network has grown to over 18,000 members across the world. These include everyone from casual observers, to behavioral scientists in training, to established academics and practitioners. To serve this diverse and growing group of people, we organize events, host a podcast, and provide resources that meet members' distinct needs. This book is another resource for practitioners, the very need for which is a strong signal of the growth and success of the field.

Why Organizations Use Behavioral Science

Charlotte Blank

U ntil as recently as a few years ago, behavioral science was barely a buzzword in the business world. The fields of behavioral economics and social psychology were burgeoning in the halls of academia, while corporations largely continued to rely on rational behavior models based on economic maximization. Then the rise of the government nudge unit revealed just how powerful the discipline can be in affecting real world behavior. As the popular media embraced behavioral science, bringing TED Talks and bestselling books on the topic to the forefront, the business world has taken notice. But that doesn't make the field any less mysterious.

Before exploring how to bring behavioral science to life in the modern organization, let's start with why the practice is making such a profound impact in firms around the world.

Insight

Fundamentally, behavioral science is a methodology for better understanding your stakeholders. Be they customers, employees, or partners, the people you need to influence are all, well, people. Behavioral science gives us the tools to uncover honest insights into how people actually behave. Not how they necessarily should behave to maximize their economic utilities, but how they really behave, in all their nuanced psychological glory.

This perspective of behavioral science as an active practice, not a turnkey solution, is a crucial distinction. By focusing on isolating the behavior of interest, running experiments and measuring actual behaviors, behavioral science teaches us not to look straightaway for answers, but for "answerable questions." When we commit to learning by observation and testable hypotheses, we challenge our own intuitions and even those of our participants, whose described preferences in traditional surveys belie their revealed preferences and true behaviors in the wild.

The results of those improved insights are material, measurable improvements to products and services that translate to higher revenue, lower costs, fewer product misfires, better experiences and loyalty, and a higher-performing organization.

Decision Making

Behavioral science helps leaders make better choices, informed by calculated risk assessment and tested assumptions. The practice of employing behavioral science methodology forces managers to be precise when defining their goals, isolating exactly what behaviors and measurable outcomes matter most in determining a successful venture. This clarity of strategy and precise focus is a fantastically valuable "side effect" of simply beginning the behavioral science journey. Further, when leaders enact the process of designing experiments and identifying data sources to measure relevant outcome variables, they tend to uncover previously unforeseen barriers to efficient learning.

So much of the work in behavioral science is in "connecting the pipes"—creating efficient back-end systems to track and measure data. This results in clarity that ultimately helps organizations not only to run experiments, but also to more effectively run their daily operations. With an efficient system in place for rapid testing of ideas, behavioral science helps leaders make swift decisions based on a broader array of options. A habit of experimentation prompts us to continuously test new ideas against the status quo—even when the status quo appears to be working just fine. It could always be better!

Culture

Why are so many leaders turning toward behavioral science in their organization? It's fun! Many of us are drawn to fields like marketing, design, and organizational development because we have a natural passion for what makes people tick. Humans are social creatures—we are interested in one another. Leaders who embrace behavioral science have an opportunity to build a culture of curious exploration.

The behaviorally-informed organization embraces behavioral science as a "verb." It empowers people to transform from "workers" to "explorers," and to find joy not only in offering solutions but also in the process of discovery. Importantly, behavioral science democratizes innovation throughout the organization, as A/B testing reveals that winning ideas can come from anywhere on the organizational chart—not only from the top. Forging a connection to academia introduces organizations to cutting edge research ideas ready for testing in a business setting—affording an edge in early adoption.

Embracing behavioral science culturally means that its methods are applied to all facets of decision making. Rather than an add on, science is a core value of the organization—it's "how we do things around here." The innovation resulting from a culture of curiosity produces better products, insights, and policies—all of which can make a difference to the bottom line as well as to the modern workplace experience.

Now is an exciting moment for the field of applied behavioral science. To take hold in the business world, organizations must apply it at scale, embracing the methodology and not only the glossary of heuristics. The purview of the science is expanding beyond present moment interventions designed to "nudge" consumers at the margin, going deeper to embrace psychological theories of motivation and identity in the human experience. As the field expands, so too will opportunities for application to transform the modern marketplace.

The Current State Of Behavioral Teams

Steve Wendel, Laurel Newman, & Zarak Khan

To better understand the range of behavioral science teams out there, and their experiences, Steve Wendel organized the largest known survey of behavioral science teams in the world.[1] This Behavioral Teams Survey was a joint project between two non-profit organizations in the field—the Behavioral Science Policy Association (BSPA) and the Action Design Network (ADN).[2] In this section, we summarize key findings from the survey and use their data to make some predictions about the future of the field.

---

[1] Please note: a version of these results was recently shared in the second edition of Designing for Behavior Change, published by O'Reilly Media, which can be found on O'Reilly's website and Amazon.com.

[2] An archived copy of the survey can be found at www.behavioralteams.com. We have also published a directory that includes the subset of organizations who were comfortable with their basic information being shared, at http://www.action-design.org/behavioral-teams-directory.

Who Is Out There

There is little doubt that behavioral science has increased in popularity and use across US businesses in the past few years. Books like *Predictably Irrational* and *Nudge* have successfully introduced behavioral science to popular audiences, and the behavioral changes described in them have led many business people to sit up and take notice. Increasingly, companies and other organizations are creating their own behavioral science teams, or are hiring behavioral scientists to work with existing teams on efforts to shape the behavior of customers, employees, or citizens.

In 2019, we launched an ongoing survey to gain a high level understanding of where and how behavioral science is used around the world. To date we have received detailed responses from 372 distinct organizations across 51 countries and augmented those detailed responses with other sources, such as web searches and social media accounts. In all, we identified a master list of 638 different groups working in the field of behavioral science. For clarity, we will refer to the group of 638 organizations as "the master list," and the sub-set of 372 organizations who responded to our survey as "survey respondents".

GEOGRAPHY

Using the master list of behavioral science teams mentioned above, we found that teams applying behavioral science to the development of products, communications and policies are heavily concentrated in five countries (among the teams with known locations): the United States (248), the United Kingdom (84), the Netherlands (34), Australia (29), India (25) and Canada (20). The extent to which behavioral science has gained popularity in the US and the UK is evident in the finding that over half of the organizations in the global directory are located in one of those two countries. However, it's worth noting that geographic diversity is on the rise: a few years ago almost all behavioral science teams were located in those two countries. Now nearly half of the organizations in our directory, including some of the most prolific groups, are located elsewhere in the world.

TEAM TYPE

The majority of behavioral teams—65% of them—are housed within companies. Behavioral units were also identified within 93 different academic institutions, as well as 69 government institutions and 58 non-profit organizations.

There is considerable diversity among the dedicated teams in organizations who filled out the survey. Roughly speaking though, we can divide them into two categories: consulting companies who apply behavioral science to external client needs, and companies that apply behavioral approaches internally to their own products and services.

An important finding here is that the majority of employment in the field, according to our survey at least, is in consulting: specifically in consulting companies in the US, UK, and Netherlands. Three of the top five largest teams in the directory are non-profit consulting organizations: the UK Behavioral Insights Team, ideas42 (in the US), and the Busara Center (based in Kenya). There are also dozens of consulting shops on the overall directory with 5 or fewer employees.[3]

For the rest of the analysis, we will focus on the survey respondents for whom we have detailed data. However, we should keep in mind that the broader field is at least 2x this size, with a strong concentration of government organizations not covered here.

---

3 Busara, while founded for academic research, now receives a majority of its funding through consulting work (Peterson, 2019)

Since the survey best represents behavioral teams in companies and non-profit organizations, unless otherwise noted we'll restrict the analysis to the primary respondent at each company or non-profit organization: 235 out of the 372 organizations that completed the survey with a known organizational type. Putting this in the context of the combined worldwide list, 53% of all known companies or non-profits with behavioral teams completed the survey.

SIZE OF THE FIELD

In total, the respondents represented corporate or non-profit teams with 1,925 members, and indicated that another 1,424 individuals applied behavioral science on other teams within their companies.[4] Combining these figures, and assuming that the survey represented 53% of the world wide total (see above), we can very roughly estimate the total worldwide employment within companies and non-profits. These teams, specifically identified as applying behavioral science, appear to employ around 6,320 people.

That number may feel surprisingly low, given the high-profile teams at Walmart, Pepsi and other major brands. However, we should be wary of generalizing from these teams: if nothing else because of the availability heuristic. And, even within these companies, the behavioral teams are generally small. Further, the largest dedicated behavioral teams in the world, including the Behavioral Insights Team in the United Kingdom and ideas42 in the United States employ less than 200 people each.[5] The largest known development agencies focusing on applied behavioral science, Innovations for Poverty Action (IPA) at

---

4 After removing entries that were clearly inaccurate, and verified as such manually.

5 As of 24 October 2019, the Behavioral Insights Team of the UK listed 181 employees, only a portion of which are actually applying behavioral science in their work (https://www.bi.team/about-us/our-people/?tab=js-tab-content-1-2) and Ideas42 listed 126 employees (https://www.ideas42.org/about-us/people/)

Northwestern and Yale and the Abdul Latif Jameel Poverty Action Lab (J-PAL) at MIT are not much larger: and many of their staff members are not directly applying behavioral science in a meaningful way or are academic professors.[6]

Given the newness of the field, this isn't too surprising. Figure 3 shows when each of the behavioral teams started. With the exception of a few pioneers in the field like Paul Slovic's Decision Research in 1976,[7] the real growth only started in 2013; 3% of teams started before the year 2000, 87% started on or after 2013.

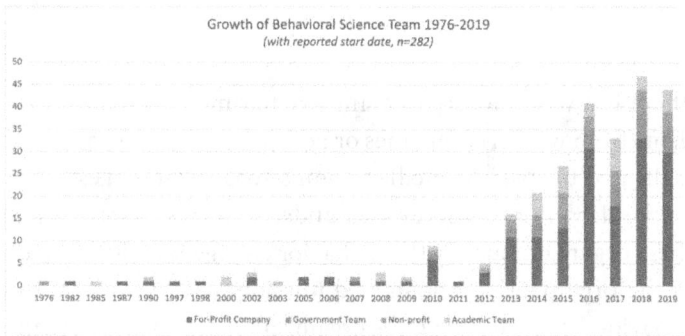

Growth of Behavioral Science Team 1976-2019
(with reported start date, n=282)

■ For-Profit Company   ■ Government Team   ■ Non-profit   ■ Academic Team

Figure 1: Starting date of behavioral science teams

That said, we can expect continued new entrants, and growth among existing teams. In the next year, the median behavioral team expects to expand by 25% (mean expected increase is 53%)—which if it held true would entail a growth of 1,580-3,349 roles next year. We should take such projected hiring with a considerable measure of salt (especially since many of these responses were given before Covid-19 hit), but nevertheless even these optimistic numbers would result in a larger, but

6 As of 24 October 2019, the J-PAL listed 294 employees worldwide, including academic professors, grant writers, etc.

7 These early pioneers are in fact real, based on manual verification of the underlying data.

generally still small, field. To put these numbers in perspective, the expected growth would result in fewer than 10,000 behavioral science workers around the globe; there are roughly 200,000 psychologists in the United States alone.

We should note, though, that survey respondents offer an incomplete source of employment projection data as all of our respondents already have a behavioral science presence, and much of the future growth will likely occur within organizations that do not.

Team Structure

There is a wide variety in team size but most of the respondents from within companies or non-profits came from small, dedicated teams. The median team size is 4; the largest team responding to our survey was under 200. Well over half of these organizations say that behavior change is explicitly part of the organization's goals and mission—often because the behavioral change team *is* the organization. For example, many small behavioral science-focused consultancies have popped up over the years.

In terms of where teams are located within the organization, and putting aside those who are in external consulting, the most common placement was data science (34%), followed by product (28%), marketing (24%), and design (23%) and HR (8%).[8]

When it comes to the individuals on the team, roughly half (52%) said that they had a formal degree in behavioral science. Among the other half, most learned through books (83%), on the job (77%), or through formal coursework (42%) or informal online learning (52%) that did not result in a degree in the field.

---

8 Percentages sum to over 100% because some roles crossed over between multiple departments. Also see note 13: these values changed significantly since the original report, because of companies being reclassified as consulting.

The dedicated teams covered by the survey, however, should be thought of as a small portion of the total population of people interested in applying behavioral science to their work. As a reference point, the Action Design Network has over 16,000 people signed up for our events around the world—many multiples of the worldwide behavioral science employment figure. Clearly most of those people are not full time behavioral scientists.

What does this mean for growth of the field? While existing behavioral science teams may continue to grow, there are many opportunities beyond that to practice behavioral science. In fact, it is the purpose of this book to help people explore that very option.

People can start a new behavioral practice within a company that does not have one, or can work as a behavioral scientist within other teams (e.g., data science, product design, or marketing). There are also opportunities for people who work in non-behavioral science roles to apply behavioral science to help them do their jobs better. It's becoming more common for UX specialists, HR professionals, designers, and customer loyalty teams to upskill by adding behavioral science principles and testing practices to their tool kits.

A Broad Range Of Application

There's no single path to starting a behavioral science team. Our respondents described a mix of bottom-up and top-down approaches—from starting a new small company specifically geared towards behavioral science (32%), to a CEO or department head driving it (20%, 16%) to individual contributors making it part of their work, and growing from there (18%).

What was uncommon however was someone outside the company convincing the company to start a team (2%). It may be that leaders are more responsive to needs or ideas of current employees, or that with no existing behavioral science team, no one sees it as their role to advocate for it. Whatever the reason, the drive to build a behavioral function appears to come most frequently from within. [9]

FOCUS AREA

What types of behavior do these teams seek to influence? Some teams are focused on particular outcomes for the individual—the most common of these being financial behavior like saving, spending and investing (54%), health behaviors (51%), education (43%) and energy use (36%).

Many also spent time on clearly company-driven outcomes of product usage (62%) and sales (52%). Respondents selected all that applied to them, and many of the companies and non-profits in the sample consult for a range of clients (resulting in percentages that sum to over 100%).

The teams use a range of techniques, as shown in Figure 4. The winner by far is social influence: social norms, social proof, etc. at 83%. The next most popular item was directing attention and shaping the choice set (both 74%). The often discussed approach of forming habits was used by 58% of respondents.

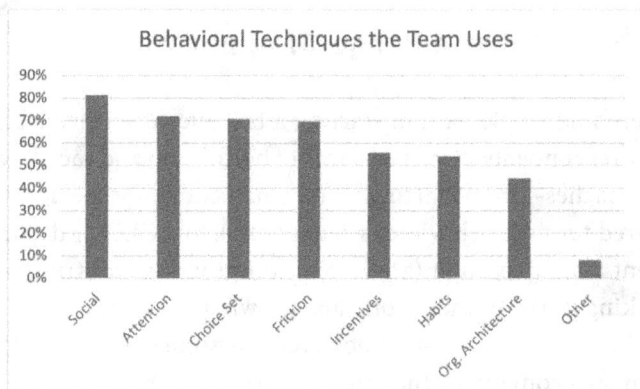

Figure 2: Techniques used by behavioral teams (respondents could choose more than one option)

9 12% of respondents replied 'other', and did not provide information that readily fit these categories.

In most cases, the target audience for these interventions did not know about them—something which raises ethical red flags, especially where the behavior is directed for the organization's benefit rather than that of the individual. 41% of respondents said that virtually no users know about the use of the behavioral interventions; 18% said a few do, and only 22% said that most people did or everyone did.

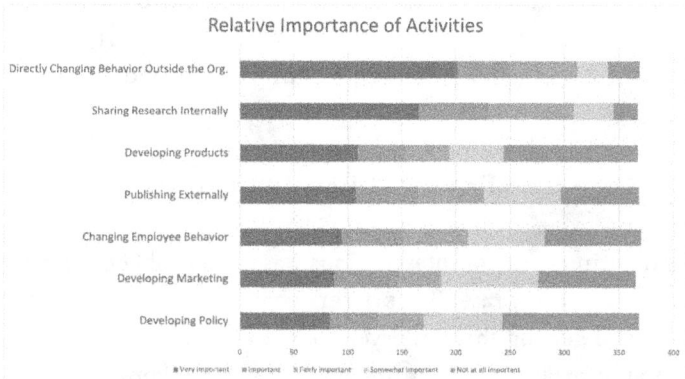

Figure 3: How important is each activity to the teams?

Respondents also reflected upon how important various aspects of their work were; the results are provided in Figure 5. Direct behavior change, not surprisingly, was consistently most important, as was sharing the results internally. Again, this analysis is limited to the companies and non-profits in the sample: the picture for academics and government agencies would be quite different.

TESTING AND EXPERIMENTATION

Given the challenges in implementation and measuring impact, it is noteworthy that 69% of respondents said their teams measured their success in terms of A/B tests or other forms of RCT. We should be cautious: the median number of experiments the teams conducted in the last twelve months was only five. While many of the teams are relatively new, that indicates either that A/B tests are not as widely used as the response might indicate, or that the teams have implemented them sparingly.

In addition to RCTs, 67% used pre-post analyses; 54% looked for direct feedback from users to gauge the effectiveness of behavioral interventions: two techniques that can be immensely valuable to gain understanding about why an intervention worked or didn't, but often aren't up to the task of measuring the impact itself effectively. Interestingly, 24% reported using statistical or machine learning techniques (beyond A/B tests).

Practical Challenges

Generating ideas for interventions was not a problem for most companies (only 14%). The primary challenges that teams faced involved getting their interventions implemented in practice (42%) or measuring their impact (41%). In the comments and subsequent interviews, respondents similarly mentioned that some of their key challenges were implementation and impact measurements.

Regarding challenges of implementation, behavioral scientists that serve as external consultants often complain that after they write their report, they move on to another project and they doubt that the client ever implements it. Internal consultants have the same complaint, except they *know* their advice wasn't really taken. Based on conversations with peers in the field, many good ideas simply aren't put into practice, whether they are behaviorally informed or not. There isn't space on the roadmap, there isn't buy-in at the appropriate levels of the company, the timing is not right, etc. This highlights a common theme of strategy consulting and an opportunity to bridge strategy and implementation within an organization.

Ironically, the opposite problem also occurs: that companies rush to implement, without measuring impact. Numerous interviewees among the survey respondents talked about their clients or their companies acting too quickly. Once the team had presented an idea, the response was: "OK, well let's do it then—why would we waste time with the test?"

This issue is not unfamiliar to applied behavioral scientists: it's difficult to simultaneously say that you have a potential solution to a known problem, and that you're not sure it will work. Stakeholders simply aren't used to hearing their experts express uncertainty. Indeed, some company leaders assume that they hire behavioral scientists *because* we have all the answers.

This is especially problematic for consultants and B2B companies whose clients expect ready-made, tried and true solutions, not ideas to test. But the reality is that impact measurements are a vital part of behavioral science. All solutions, derived from behavioral science or not, could fail to have an effect or, worse, backfire. It's just that behavioral teams are generally more comfortable saying so, and more cautious about making claims without solid empirical evidence to back them up.

PART II

PRACTICE AREAS

The previous section introduced various ways behavioral science is used across an organization. In the following section, we have asked leaders in behavioral science with practical experience in their respective disciplines to help explain how they use behavioral science in that area, the tangible steps they suggest to integrate it, and the limitations one should anticipate.

Employee Culture And Human Resources

Laurel Newman

B ehavioral science can be used to strengthen and improve a variety of Practice Areas across an organization. Laurel Newman explains its application to Employee Culture and Human Resources.

How a Behavioral Scientist Contributes

US companies spend billions of dollars each year on compensation and related programs designed to attract, retain, and motivate employees. HR efforts to improve employee experience and performance generally fall into such categories as:

- Health and well-being (healthy diet, hand washing, etc.)
- Learning and development
- Goal setting and performance management
- Compensation, including benefits, bonuses, perks, incentives & rewards

HR leaders are generally highly motivated to improve these programs and their associated outcomes. They often do not have the full skill set, however, that's needed to do so. Most people's assumptions about human behavior and decision making are outdated and incomplete. This leads to the design of programs that are well-intentioned, but that fail to capture people's attention, that overlook constraints on people's time or ability, or that tap into the wrong kind of motivation. Behavioral scientists can help here by guiding the design of programs to ensure that they work for "real humans" (who are often busy, overwhelmed, and "predictably irrational"). Behavioral scientists are also well-informed of the literature surrounding motivation and behavior. We can draw from hundreds of behavioral science principles (think loss aversion, social proof, ego depletion, etc.) to help improve programs by infusing behavioral design.

Behavioral scientists' mastery of the research process can also prove helpful. Demonstrating the impact of your initiatives requires that we assess the effects that they have on key outcomes like workplace engagement, retention, and performance. As scientists, we can design pilot tests that assess the impact of a new program or intervention so we'll know whether it's worth abandoning or scaling up throughout the business. And when pilot tests are not possible, we can work with data and business teams to ensure that the right metrics are collected before, during, and after interventions to give us some insight into their effects. Another benefit of our research skills is that we can dig into the research on particular areas of interest (pro-social rewards, health behaviors, relationship building) and can evaluate the results with a careful eye. Many headlines you see in popular publications or on social media are overblown or fail to consider boundaries around the effect (when would it *not* work?). To fully understand what a body of research has shown, you must read and evaluate the credibility of the original research with a trained eye.

Those are a few of the most important ways behavioral scientists can contribute to any business area, including but not limited to HR and employee experience. As the concepts are largely theoretical, the remainder of this chapter will provide concrete examples of how behavioral scientists might support specific business goals.

Most readers will be familiar with the idea of *nudging*, which involves minor tweaks to the environment that lead to an increase in the desired behavior, often with the whole process occurring outside the target's awareness. One of the most common uses of behavioral science involves nudging momentary behaviors such as getting a flu shot or signing up for your 401K. Efforts may also extend to broader behavioral patterns such as exercising regularly or completing a series of training sessions. To influence longer-term patterns of behavior, we must go beyond nudges and either make lasting, structural changes to the environment or change something within the person (e.g., by creating a habit or increasing their intrinsic motivation to do it). Behavioral scientists help design environments that do this. For example, a technology company who wants their employees to take a new approach to customer service might redesign their environment to include more autonomy (choice of how to resolve customer complaints), mastery (recognition for their successes), social connection (small group meetings to support one another) and purpose (how their services allow customers to accomplish their own important business), all of which have been shown to increase intrinsic motivation. We simply cannot nudge people into being more intrinsically motivated.

Within HR, much of the action for impacting employee engagement also lies within areas like bonuses and rewards,

recognition, learning and development, goal setting, and progress feedback. Behavioral scientists can help design programs,
processes, and products that improve the effectiveness of all of
these functions. For example, we can help develop or select a
recognition platform that follows best practices for giving meaningful recognition. We may be able to work with data scientists
to find important behavioral patterns (Is your naturally occurring recognition activity gender biased? Is recognition from a
skip level superior more impactful for retention than feedback
from peers or direct supervisors?). We can pilot test traditional
training sessions against shorter, more frequent micro-learning
sessions or team based trainings, which may increase account-
ability and focus. Or we can weigh in on employee-focused
software platforms before they are purchased to make sure the
company invests in products that work for "real humans" and
for the needs of your specific organization.

Behavioral scientists can also help with employee engagement and performance by assisting colleagues outside of HR.
For example, by working with executives on how to build a
culture that attracts, engages, and retains the best employees.
One well-known exemplar here is Google's food program, which
is really an employee engagement program in disguise. The
original goal was to create environments that would increase
"casual collisions." These are the happenstance interactions that
build relationships, transfer tacit knowledge, and lead to bright
ideas and innovations. The food program was masterful in its
combination of intrinsic motivators (delicious gourmet food
in a beautiful setting with interesting colleagues) and extrinsic
motivators (it's all free—you'd be a fool not to go!). If one out of
every 100 collisions yields something amazing, why not create
100 times more of them? Especially if the consolation prize—a
free delicious lunch with colleagues that does not change the
world—still builds social connection and makes people love

their jobs more. A project of this scope requires buy-in from many stakeholders, including executives outside of HR, and these folks will expect that you'll collect data and report back on the benefits.

How To Integrate Behavioral Science

Typically issues of employee engagement and experience are centralized in HR. However, some companies are making an effort to extend responsibility to other areas (executive teams and direct managers), or are expanding HR to include researchers and analysts. Wherever a business places the responsibility for employee satisfaction, engagement, and retention, that would be an appropriate place to add a behavioral scientist to the team. Regardless of where they are located, behavioral scientists must have the ability to access key employee data, such as performance and review information and employee satisfaction ratings. They should also be able to collect baseline-level qualitative and quantitative data to better understand employee sentiment.

To go beyond analyzing baseline data (what is and isn't working right now?) and uncover new insights that improve employee experience (what else could be we doing and how can we know it works?), they should also have the ability to guide leadership on potential changes that may boost motivation, ability, and engagement and to test the impact of at least some of them. Testing can take the form of pilot or larger scale experiments and quasi experiments. Where experiments are not possible, we can conduct careful analyses of how key outcomes change before vs. after an intervention, taking care to be tentative about internal and external validity inferences.

The Limitations Of Behavioral Science

There is enormous potential for behavioral science—and psychological research more broadly—to be applied towards improving employee well-being and attracting and retaining top talent. However, the impact you can have in any specific role will depend on several things.

To be successful, you'll absolutely need access to data and support for at least some level of intervention, experimentation, and measurement. Ideally, you'd work on a team with other behavioral scientists, data scientists, and HR professionals who are familiar with your organization's current investments in employee engagement (compensation and rewards, learning and development, etc.). A single behavioral scientist may be effective at designing small nudges, but would probably have little influence over costlier endeavors like incentive programs, professional development, or even pilot testing innovative hiring practices.

Finally, the effectiveness of these initiatives will depend more than anything on the will of executive leadership. Most companies want to build an amazing culture, but few are willing to invest the resources it takes to do so.

Executives who are overly focused on short term gains and losses, who are risk averse, or who subscribe to narrow "carrot and stick" beliefs about motivation will be resistant to real change. If you find yourself in such an environment, you'll have to look for low-cost solutions. For example, sometimes well-timed messages that tap into purpose or communicate progress towards a collective goal can be inspiring and cost nothing but a few minutes of time and effort. Companies who view employees as assets to be optimized may also be resistant to the idea that employee motivation and engagement is worth attending to, much less investing in.

However, as behavioral science and data science merge with the world of HR, culture leaders will emerge because of their ability to "humanize their optimize." That is, to optimize the performance of their employees not by whittling away at their autonomy, growth, and other human needs, but by strategically investing in them and quantifying the impact.

Consumer And Market Research

Namika Sagara

B ehavioral science can be used to strengthen and improve a variety of Practice Areas across an organization. Namika Sagara explains its application to Consumer and Market Research.

How A Behavioral Scientist Contributes

As organizations attempt to gather information about target markets and customers, behavioral science can be leveraged by organizations to gain a deeper and more holistic understanding of consumers by applying behavioral principles and frameworks in various areas including but not limited to:

- Intent vs. action gaps
- Automatic and habitual behavior (e.g., how they are formed and disrupted, how long they last)

- Emotional and motivational drivers behind behaviors (e.g., understanding why consumers do what they do)
- Non-conscious factors influencing consumer decision-making process and choices

There are two major ways behavioral scientists can contribute to understanding of consumers and other stakeholders. One is to apply behavioral frameworks and principles to 'traditional' market research (see Section 1 below). Another is to leverage existing behavioral science literature to better understand consumers, without conducting primary research of your own (see Section 2 below).

SECTION 1: APPLYING BEHAVIORAL SCIENCE TO 'TRADITIONAL' MARKET RESEARCH

Behavioral science can be applied to many different areas of market research including but not limited to:

- Copy, claim and ad test
- Pack test
- Attitude and usage test
- Consumer segmentations
- Various tracking programs
- Other custom surveys (both qualitative and quantitative)

Behavioral science can be used to optimize the basic consumer research design, such as how we ask questions and in what order. Such framing effects have been well-documented in judgment and decision-making research. In addition, a change in the order in which the questions and answers are presented can lead to a change in the responses due to the effect of priming.

Unfortunately, there is often not a 'neutral' way of framing or ordering questions. Therefore, it is important to think about how consumers actually think and behave in the real-world, and try to mimic this in a research environment.

Another way to apply behavioral science to market research is to leverage behavioral frameworks. For example, Regulatory Focus Theory has shown that people tend to have two different motivations: promotion mindset and prevention mindset.[10][11] Consumers with a promotion mindset are more motivated to achieve their goals and desires and to become their ideal selves (e.g., the best version of yourself). In contrast, a prevention mindset is when consumers' motivation is centered around fulfilling their duties and obligations, and they are more motivated by their 'ought' self (e.g., the kind of person who you think you should be). These underlying motivations can influence desire for different products and services, but also how they experience these products and what they remember about the experiences.

By understanding deeper motivations, you can gain insights not only into what consumers say they do but also into why they behave the way they do.

SECTION 2: USING BEHAVIORAL SCIENCE LITERATURE TO UNDERSTAND CONSUMERS

As many readers may know, behavioral science can tell you a lot about how people process information. For example, we know that framing can lead a consumer to be more loss averse. It is true that the intensity of loss aversion differs for each individual, and that there are contextual effects. However, the guideline that certain framing leads consumers to be loss averse generally holds across different contexts. This is one example of knowledge that behavioral scientists can provide without additional primary

---

10 Higgins, E. Tory. "Beyond pleasure and pain." American psychologist 52.12 (1997): 1280.

11 Higgins, E. Tory. "Promotion and prevention: Regulatory focus as a motivational principle." Advances in experimental social psychology. Vol. 30. Academic Press, 1998. 1-46.

research. Because behavioral science literature can teach you about how consumers process information, and what drives consumers' behavior, it can guide you towards a deeper and more nuanced understanding of consumer behavior.

By leveraging thousands of published principles, behavioral scientists can help you understand how your consumers process the information you provide via different platforms, such as ads, copy, website, package, and in-store signage. Using the example of Regulatory Focus Theory discussed above, behavioral scientists can identify if and how your marketing collaterals are non-consciously communicating product benefits in a promotion or prevention way (or both).

These insights are not limited to the usage of language; it also applies to how different stimuli, such as images, color, and location on the page. For example, products placed at the bottom of the ad or package are non-consciously perceived to be heavier.[12] And more subtle effects such as borders around text and logos can provide more structure and reduce certain psychological barriers (e.g. uncertainty about product information.[13] Consumers usually cannot articulate the impact of these factors when asked in surveys or interviews because they are unaware that these principles exist.

Two key approaches for behavioral science to contribute to a better understanding of consumers are discussed above. Each has its pros and cons, and one may fit better with the needs and resources your organization has. However, the most optimal approach for holistic understanding is to use a combination of both since each will provide different insights.

---

12 Deng, Xiaoyan, and Barbara E. Kahn. "Is your product on the right side? The "location effect" on perceived product heaviness and package evaluation." Journal of Marketing Research 46.6 (2009): 725-738.

13 Cutright, Keisha M. "The beauty of boundaries: When and why we seek structure in consumption." Journal of Consumer Research 38.5 (2012): 775-790.

How To Integrate Behavioral Science

In order to integrate behavioral science into primary research, you can collaborate with behavioral scientists on various research projects. As discussed above, behavioral scientists can review surveys and discussion guides to ensure that the wording, the order of questions, and answer options are appropriately framed.

In addition, behavioral scientists can help you select the most effective behavioral framework to use in research based on research goals and business challenges. They can then apply the appropriate framework to guide the design of surveys and interview guides.

For example, imagine you have a project assessing sunscreen usage. Traditional market research may ask if and how often consumers use sunscreen, and what brand they prefer. Behavioral science can go above and beyond what consumers (intend to) do, and uncover underlying motivations that customers are unaware of. By using the behavioral framework of Regulatory Focus Theory, you can measure your consumers' general tendencies to have a promotion versus prevention mindset,[14] and you can measure to what extent consumers believe that your products will fulfill their promotional or preventative mindset. Similarly, you can determine whether consumers have either mindset specific to your product (vs. general tendencies). For example, do your consumers use sunscreen to free them up to have the most exciting and fun vacation they can (ideal self)? Or do they use sunscreen to fulfill their responsibility as parents and to protect themselves and their kids from sunburn (ought self)? The behavior of sunscreen usage might be the same (e.g.,

---

14 Higgins, E. Tory, et al. "Achievement orientations from subjective histories of success: Promotion pride versus prevention pride." European Journal of Social Psychology 31.1 (2001): 3-23.

they always apply sunscreen when they are out in the sun) but the motivation behind the usage is different.

This is important because you can apply these insights to your marketing strategies and tactics. For example, if research tells you that your consumers use your products to fulfill promotion mindset, then your marketing strategies should communicate through different language and images how your products can help achieve their goals and desires and become their ideal self. If research tells you that your consumers use your products to fulfill a prevention mindset, then your marketing strategies should communicate how products can help avoid negatives and become their 'ought' self.

The Limitations Of Behavioral Science

More often than not, behavioral science is unfortunately seen only as a methodology or as an 'add-on' to the research processes. In order to reach its full potential, it's critical that behavioral science is fully integrated throughout the consumer insights process, with close collaboration between market researchers and behavioral scientists. Tactically speaking, research that fully integrates behavioral science may require more resources, especially as research teams start to learn how to incorporate behavioral science. Therefore, buy-in from leadership is essential.

Finally, companies often hire behavioral scientists with the mistaken impression that they already know exactly how to optimize behavior or marketing. Behavioral science does provide a granular understanding of people and contexts, which will enable you to take a smarter and more informed approach. But behavioral science is not a silver bullet. While we have more informed ideas because of our expertise, we still must try those ideas out and measure their results.

Marketing

Erik Johnson

B ehavioral science can be used to strengthen and improve a variety of Practice Areas across an organization. Erik Johnson explains its application to Marketing.

How A Behavioral Scientist Contributes

At its core, marketing is a simple discipline. Businesses have products or services that they believe solve consumers' problems, and marketers work to connect those sellers with potential buyers.

In an economically rational world, this would be a very simple task. Rational consumers would always buy the most technically advanced product within their precisely defined budget, so marketers would simply need to share their products' technical specifications and price and watch the sales come in.

The real world is far from rational, though. Consumer choice is often, if not usually, irrational. Status signals sell better than usefulness, so we buy luxury products costing 20 times their competitors and put it on credit cards with no clear plan of paying it back. We buy low risk products that are "good enough" rather than optimize for technical advancement. With so many choices and demands on our attention, we fall for slick branding and clever marketing that captivates our lizard brain.

Consumers are irrational, so effective marketing must be irrational, too. While marketing's greatest minds, like David Ogilvy and Claude Hopkins, usually demonstrate a keen understanding of psychology, they are the exceptions, not the rule, and most relied on intuition and experience in the absence of extensive study into consumer decision-making. Modern marketers face no such dilemma. Behavioral science has studied the eccentricities of consumer psychology for decades, and its rich knowledge set should be an essential part of marketing strategy.

Behavioral science can be incorporated into marketing strategy in a variety of ways. The psychology of the target consumer should be the starting point. Like any other business strategy, marketing fails when it's insular and top down rather than customer-focused and bottom up. Marketers should understand the needs and challenges of their customers independent of the product or service being sold and use that as the foundation of strategy. For example, marketing channels should be chosen based on the consumer's preferences, rather than what the business typically uses. As a bonus, such deep customer knowledge improves the consistency of brand experience. This understanding can be developed with the tools of market research and analysis of the consumer segment's past behavior and preferences. This can also be done in collaboration with the product team's user research efforts.

With a sufficient understanding of the target consumer, marketers can then leverage the vast behavioral science literature relevant to their problems and needs to develop messaging and campaigns. There's no need to reinvent the wheel when there is decades of research and data to utilize. A literature review of both academic and industry research relevant to the consumer's needs will uncover valuable ideas that can be adopted and tested as part of the strategy.

"Testing" is key here. Marketing often invests heavily in researching what might happen instead of measuring what's actually happening. Behavioral scientists do the opposite. They know that what consumers say is often much different than what they do and that we often have no idea what will work until it's properly tested. Marketing strategy should be developed as a series of hypotheses to be tested and evaluated, not as a final blueprint based on gut feeling. As a bonus, testing continuously builds the knowledge base that forms the foundation of the strategy. Behavioral scientists can build and execute measurement systems that do just that, making marketing efforts more effective and efficient.

There are many methods for testing and measurement in marketing. Marketers should first define two factors: how much time they have to execute a test and what level of certainty they need from the resulting data. Ultimately, testing is a tool for reducing uncertainty. The more advanced and precise a test is, the more confident a marketer can be that its result will hold true in a full rollout. Such tests are difficult to execute, though, and in many cases the tradeoff between effort and outcomes isn't worth it.

When time is short and the need for certainty is low, tests that serve as a simple gut check may suffice. Simple user tests with participants outside of the company (ideally, in your customer's demographic) can spot big issues quickly and give a sense of consumer reaction. Traditional market research methods like customer interviews or surveys can also serve this purpose.

When there is more time and demand for certainty, more sophisticated data-driven methods can be utilized, such as quantitative usability testing of campaigns. Staggered rollouts, where the campaign is rolled out to a small subset of customers as a test group, can also be done.

When time available and need for certainty are the highest, randomized controlled trials—typically called A/B tests in the business world—are the best tool. They are the most precise of testing methods and reduce uncertainty the most, but are also challenging to execute correctly and not feasible in many situations.

Thus, A/B tests should only be executed when some key conditions are in place. For one, an experienced behavioral or data scientist should lead their design and execution. It's all too common for marketing departments to leave A/B testing in the hands of digital marketers lacking sufficient training in statistics and experimental design, leading to poorly run tests that result in incomplete data for smart decision-making. Second, for most companies, they should be reserved for the most strategic questions impacting marketing strategy. Properly executed A/B testing requires strict conditions that are challenging for most businesses to accommodate, so they should be deployed to answer important questions that benefit from a high degree of certainty in their answers. In one example, music streaming service Pandora ran an experiment that lasted nearly two years with 35 million users to determine the optimal volume of advertising[15].

The exception to this rule is companies with very high volumes of customers and advanced data infrastructures. Companies like Google, Facebook, and Amazon have hundreds of millions of customers to test on, and can afford to deploy A/B tests with more regularity.

Consistent testing pays off beyond each individual use case,

---

15 "Pandora tested listeners' tolerance for advertisements by ...." 1 May. 2018, https:// qz.com/1261831/pandora-tested-listeners-tolerance-for-advertisements-by-experimenting-on-35-million-users/. Accessed 21 Oct. 2020.

as well, by building the knowledge base of consumer insights. The behavioral foundation of the marketing strategy can continually by enriched by findings from frequent testing.

How To Integrate Behavioral Science

Behavioral science should be baked into the DNA of marketing efforts. Start by integrating a behavioral scientist to the marketing team and involve them in all strategic discussions. Having a behavioral lens applied to your planning will begin to uncover those irrational opportunities that are likely being missed.

A behavioral scientist should also be heavily involved in planning the execution of campaigns. Specifically, they should advise on how to test your ideas and evaluate their impact. They should be responsible for executing those tactics and interpreting the findings for the rest of the team.

Finally, let them take the lead on creating an environment where behavioral science can thrive naturally. They should train other marketers on behavioral methods and help them apply it to their work. More crucially, give them the resources to build the proper infrastructure. This means proper measurement, experimentation, and research tools, as well as people who can manage and execute them.

The Limitations Of Behavioral Science

Behavioral science is not a magic bullet that can transform your marketing overnight. The marketing world is riddled with examples of simple A/B tests that drastically improve conversion rates with minor changes, but these are rare and often misleading. Further, most A/B tests are limited to one-time behaviors, such as booking a room online or signing up for a newsletter. Development of a strong brand presence and deep loyalty with customers requires a pattern of investment from the brand in their customers; it can't be built through any single digital experience, even if it has won the A/B test. Behavioral marketing is an investment, not an overnight success.

In making this investment, here's how to know you're on the right track. First, ensure that you have high quality information to work with. Behavioral science cannot make up for bad data. Without investing in tools and people that can upgrade your data and research infrastructure, you'll only be scratching the surface of potential. To do that, organizations should see where they stand in three areas: data quality, analysis capabilities, and research tools and talent.

The first focuses on the fundamentals of data collection. Data engineers should dig into the infrastructure to confirm it's capturing the information you care about in a reliable way. This includes the development and ongoing maintenance of data-bases and installation of analytics tools that create a front-end view of behavior. An important, but often overlooked, aspect of this is being able to accurately measure important behaviors outside of the typical marketing funnel. It's not enough to just know whether someone engaged with an email campaign. You need to know if they eventually bought something, too, and whether they continued to do so. Doing this may involve collaborating with other functions across the organization, but is a worthwhile effort to understand the entire behavioral path of customers and full ROI of marketing efforts.

Next, make sure you have a team that can make sense of the data. Analysts and data scientists can tease out interesting patterns of behavior and play a crucial part in documenting the story of your audience. Such analysis is critical for well-informed hypotheses and measuring the impact of changes.

Finally, optimize this infrastructure with the tools and skill sets of research. Software to test hypotheses is a must. Ideally, this would mean A/B testing via tools like Optimizely or VWO, but less rigorous testing is important, too. When time or resources won't accommodate a randomized experiment, the traditional tools of market research are valuable. Whether user testing campaign drafts, surveying potential audiences, or running prototypes in Mechanical Turk, many tools can serve as a gut check to hypotheses and acquire valuable feedback.

Other limitations emerge from organizational structure and culture. Beyond a proper data and research infrastructure, buy-in from key decision makers can make or break a behavioral marketing effort. It is not uncommon for major companies to hire experts to come in, conduct research, and unearth an important finding about their business, only for that information to be wasted. Without a culture of data-driven decision-making starting at the top, valuable findings will languish unused at the whim of HiPPOs (highest paid person in the office).

Further, if behavioral science is left below the view of key decision-makers, it will likely be unable to even tackle meaningful problems. Quick wins like an A/B test increasing opens to an email campaign may get attention initially, but bigger strategic wins should be the goal. For those to happen, behavioral science must be in the conversation with leadership.

Product Management

Kristen Berman

B ehavioral science can be used to strengthen and improve a variety of Practice Areas across an organization. Kristen Berman, co-founder of Irrational Labs, explains its application to Product Management.

How A Behavioral Scientist Contributes

A product manager's role is to oversee the research required to prioritize, design and develop the features and go-to market plan that will make a product a success. Doing this well requires a deep understanding of both the customer and market forces. This is where behavioral science comes in. A behavioral scientist is helpful at all stages of the product development cycle:

Ideation: A behavioral scientist goes beyond conducting typical focus groups and customer interviews. They take a deeper look at customer psychology by doing a 'behavioral diagnosis', which includes collecting data about existing behaviors; doing a literature review of the space; and mapping out the user's environment of decision-making. A behavioral scientist thus helps a PM go beyond what customers 'say' they want, and instead reveals the underlying psychology driving a person.

Research: After completing a behavioral diagnosis, the behavioral scientist partners with the PM to narrow down the long list of possible new features or solutions. Behavioral scientists are experts at isolating a key assumption and designing a rapid test to see whether it's true. A behavioral scientist pushes the team to avoid relying on their intuition for product decisions. They bring in rigorous research methods such as quantitative studies or clever prototypes to help uncover what actually has market viability.

Design: Rather than thinking in terms of 'solutions', a behavioral scientist thinks in terms of behaviors. What is the uncomfortably specific behavior you should design our feature or product around? For example, if you're an education startup, you may want people to finish your online courses or if you're a healthtech company you may want people to log their daily exercise in your app. A behavioral scientist helps the PM and design team home in on this behavior, then design small ways to drive customers *to* that behavior. Behavioral science is about the details—people make different decisions depending on the design and context of an experience. A behavioral scientist partners with designers to ensure that all those small details (from copy to onboarding flow) align with the broader customer psychology.

Launch: A behavioral scientist works with engineering and the PM to design the 'launch and learn' roll-out strategy. This includes generating an experimental design; the team's hypothesis on which version will win; the sample size, conversion, and effect size; and how long the experiment will run. They work alongside the data team to publish their data analysis plan prior to launching, and they're frontline in terms of promoting both successful and failed experiments so the rest of the company can learn from the experience. They also help design the knowledge management system for reporting results to ensure that the long-term product strategy builds on the incremental learning journey.

How To Integrate Behavioral Science

There are two recommended approaches to integrating behavioral science into product management. One, have a behavioral scientist as the actual PM; or two, have the behavioral scientist report to the PM.

The first option is ideal for products and services that are focused on behavior change problems. For example, PMs at places like Headspace (meditation app), Chime (savings app) or Classdojo (classroom learning) should have a background in behavioral science. Kelvin Kwong, the VP of Product at Big Health, a mental health and digital therapeutic, is an experienced behavioral PM and works to embed behavior change models and nudges directly into their roadmap.

For products and services that aren't directly tied to behavior change, the PM should hire a behavioral scientist to have on their team. It's important that the behavioral scientists have a direct reporting line to the PM (vs. being put in the research section of the organization).

Behavioral scientists work across all stages of product development—from concept to code. Reporting directly to the PM will help ensure behavioral insights are not relegated to only one part of the process.

The Limitations Of Behavioral Science

There are two primary considerations for PMs in the application of behavioral science:

Context matters: Our decision-making is strongly influenced by our environment (situation/context). Because of that, it's difficult to drag and drop behavioral insights from one domain to another. PMs must live and breathe the *process* of behavioral science vs. solely the psychology insights. The process is about testing your intuition via quantitative studies, controlled trials or at minimum slow rollouts. It's about leading with a key behavior and hypothesis, and being willing to change your mind when it's proven wrong. This point is even more important if you're building a new startup or product where the context is likely different than ones that have existed before.

It's an art and a science: Behavioral science exposes key psychological principles that affect your users (and potential users) as they engage with your products. Which of these principles is the most important for your customers? Which should you tackle first? In a perfect world you'd go through each in a systematic way to determine the most important levers. Of course, no product team has time or money for that! So when creating new products and modifying existing ones, you'll need to make prioritization decisions with less data than is ideal. To facilitate this, we pick a key behavior (this is critical!) and then we focus on removing the barriers to this key behavior. Barriers can be logistical frictions (i.e., too many steps or choices) or psychological frictions (i.e., information aversion or attention). Only after the biggest barriers are removed, do we focus on the 3rd B—benefits. We add more immediate benefits (like social proof or points) or amplify existing benefits (your current value proposition)

Building successful products can be a rigorous process but it's also one infused with creativity, non-linear thinking and bold risk-taking. To successfully incorporate behavioral science into product management, you'll need a dash of art to go with your science.

Innovation

Zarak Khan

B ehavioral science can be used to strengthen and improve
a variety of Practice Areas across an organization. Zarak
Khan explains its application to Innovation.

How A Behavioral Scientist Contributes

Compared to decades ago, organizations today start up, grow,
and die at a much more rapid pace. Because of technology and
globalization, organizations no longer compete only with local
rivals. To grow and maintain success, they must compete against
other organizations around the world—in physical and digital
space—and they must win. Companies that are able to do this
for a long period of time recognize the fast pace with which
their business must change; not only in response to changing
market needs but often in *anticipation* of them. This is exem-
plified by recent shifts in the makeup of corporate innovation
portfolios towards new business models and distributions
channels. Having an organized team or initiative dedicated to
innovation is all but a requirement.

Innovation involves a series of important behaviors: going out of one's way to learn about business challenges and market trends, proposing ideas to improve the business, and moving those ideas forward to implementation. Innovation involves more than behavior, though. It requires environments that spark and nurture bright ideas. It requires building relationships across business areas so that these ideas will be better informed and supported. It involves social influence: gathering support for ideas that might be initially rejected by people who have only known—or who benefit from—the status quo.

To put it simply, innovation initiatives involve behaviors— but also thoughts, emotions, and relationships—of people throughout an organization. Because of this, innovation initiatives are usually more successful if they are informed by a behavioral scientist.

To know how a behavioral scientist contributes to innovation, it's helpful to first have a framework for thinking about innovation work within an organization. Broadly, innovation activities typically fall within the following three areas:

1. **Looking Innovative:** initiatives, communications, and programs that are designed to make the organization appear innovative to potential clients, competitors, and employees. For example, sponsoring an open hackathon with university students.
2. **Feeling Innovative:** initiatives, communications, and programs that are targeted internally at current employees to reassure them that they work at an innovative organization. For example, hosting an internal speaker series with famous thought leaders.
3. **Being Innovative:** initiatives, communications, and programs that are designed to increase the number of ideas

that an organization generates, evaluates, and develops to have a material impact on its financial success.

In this chapter, we will focus on Being Innovative. Looking and Feeling Innovative are important functions as well, as they showcase the success of your efforts to the marketplace and help facilitate an innovative culture. Companies' efforts to look innovative to external stakeholders should originate from marketing and branding teams. Efforts to help employees feel that they work for an innovative company are generally organized by HR leaders. Behavioral scientists can assist with these efforts by working on or with those teams, as described in the Marketing and Employee Culture sections, respectively.

Being innovative consists of five functions: generating, assessing, designing, launching and scaling ideas. Things like hackathons, crowdsourcing, startup incubators, and accelerators are all examples of tactics that align to these broad functions. Behavioral scientists' expertise in shaping human perception and behavior can support all of these.

A behavioral scientist can also help think through and align incentives within the organization to facilitate innovation. This is relevant throughout the process, but its merit becomes especially apparent for certain types of ideas in the launch and scale phases. A quick detour into innovation theory can be helpful here.

Ideas can be triaged into three broad categories: incremental, adjacent, and transformational. This is important because based on where an idea falls, it is treated quite differently.

Incremental innovations are small and simple improvements or tweaks made to a product or strategy. These innovations are closely tied to the core business, unlike adjacent or transformational innovation. They are typically managed within a business unit—paid for by the BU and completed with the team's existing resources. This is because it's usually more difficult to have an external team build and then reintegrate it. Incremental innovation is often seen as a natural evolution of doing good business. The level of investment and the level of risk are generally fairly low, so it's the least likely to bump up against fatal friction. The key goal is to build environments that encourage people to see business challenges as "their problem to solve," and that help make the process motivating and easy for people whose main job is not innovation.

Adjacent innovations leverage something a company or product already does well in a new or innovative way. They are less closely tied to the core business than incremental innovations. And the cost and responsibilities are often shared between business units and a corporate team—typically because it's a bigger investment and a longer time horizon. One of the bigger challenges here is underfunding and over-reliance on a business unit to accomplish adjacent innovation by itself.

Transformational innovations are the most long-term mode of innovation, which companies often find too risky to invest in. This often involves entering an entirely new market segment, using a new distribution strategy, or testing a new business model. Sometimes those new business models threaten to cannibalize the existing business. Because of that threat, the risk and cost involved, and the long time horizon, they are most often led by a corporate team. They also experience the most resistance, as fully embracing a new business model not only threatens the existing business, but the jobs of the very people who must approve it.

A behavioral scientist can triage ideas into these categories, which helps ensure that they receive the proper treatment and that good, disruptive ideas are not prematurely killed by the current incentive structure within the organization that protects the status quo.

How To Integrate Behavioral Science

From a strategic perspective, a behavioral scientist can help design your innovation infrastructure and processes in a way that facilitates key behaviors that move innovations from idea to impact.

For starters, having a process in the first place! One of the key tenets of behavioral science is that if you want someone to exhibit a behavior more frequently, make it easier for them to do. An innovation process and the thoughtful introduction of some tools can decrease friction at key moments to make it easier to share and shape ideas at the top of the innovation funnel.

There are many innovation process maps, but here is a generic one that can serve as a starting point for most organizations:

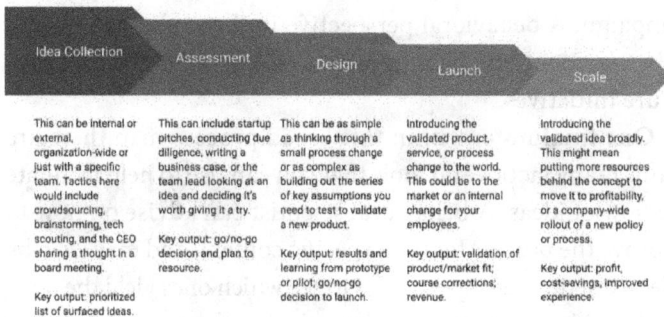

Idea Collection	Assessment	Design	Launch	Scale
This can be internal or external, organization-wide or just with a specific team. Tactics here would include crowdsourcing, brainstorming, tech scouting, and the CEO sharing a thought in a board meeting.	This can include startup pitches, conducting due diligence, writing a business case, or the team lead looking at an idea and deciding it's worth giving it a try.	This can be as simple as thinking through a small process change or as complex as building out the series of key assumptions you need to test to validate a new product.	Introducing the validated product, service, or process change to the world. This could be to the market or an internal change for your employees.	Introducing the validated idea broadly. This might mean putting more resources behind the concept to move it to profitability, or a company-wide rollout of a new policy or process.
Key output: prioritized list of surfaced ideas.	Key output: go/no-go decision and plan to resource.	Key output: results and learning from prototype or pilot; go/no-go decision to launch.	Key output: validation of product/market fit; course corrections; revenue.	Key output: profit, cost-savings, improved experience.

As ideas enter and move through the innovation process, a behavioral scientist can help you build your infrastructure for operational transparency. Incubating innovations takes time—and a common concern from innovators is "I shared my ideas with you and nothing seems to have happened." Greater transparency and showing the work going on behind the scenes can increase people's patience with the process and confidence in the outcome.

And while the idea collection phase may have very low friction to make it as easy as possible to surface ideas, as you assess ideas, a behavioral scientist may recommend adding some friction back into the process. Most of the time when we talk about friction, we talk about reducing friction to make it easier for someone to do a desired behavior. In some cases, though, it can actually be beneficial to increase friction. That's the case in an assessment phase, where there is a need to ensure that the most promising ideas, with sponsorship within the business, move forward to design. This might be a requirement to create a business case, a pitch session, or some other mechanism to vet ideas.

After assessment, ideas that move forward to design and launch can benefit from a close read of the Product Management section of this book. Similarly, when scaling a successful idea a behavioral scientist might advise an HR initiative or Marketing campaign. A behavioral perspective in these phases can lead to better adoption, measurement and learnings that improve future initiatives.

One final note: within this broad process map there are many, many tactics and tools that you can use to help facilitate the flow of ideas. A behavioral scientist can advise on how to improve the process for your specific context, and may even be able to test different approaches to see which ones yield the most and best ideas. For instance, introducing a pre-mortem to the assessment phase, or testing out different balances of intrinsic and extrinsic motivators to galvanize participation in ideation.

Wherever there is a key decision or action, a behavioral scientist can assess and help improve the outcome.

The Limitations Of Behavioral Science

A behavioral scientist can help create infrastructure that supports innovation and can improve innovative ideas. They still must work in partnership with other key areas of the organization to realize that vision and bring innovations from concept to reality.

In particular, a behavioral scientist supporting innovation needs to be closely aligned to strategy, with access and input from key decision makers. Without that, innovation initiatives run the risk of wasting time, energy, and money to produce something that nobody wants or needs.

Behavioral science does not predict the future. It is, however, often useful to think about behavior as a core element of a successful venture. That focus, and expertise in behavioral science, can improve innovative ventures but they are still subject to broader forces that may exist in the market or within the organization.

Data Science And Measurement

Greg Szwartz

B ehavioral science can strengthen and improve a variety of Practice Areas across an organization. Greg Szwartz explains its connection to Data Science, and the partnership that should be developed between data and behavioral scientists in designing solutions that improve business outcomes.

How A Behavioral Scientist Contributes

Focusing on key behaviors brings data and behavioral scientists together (and improves project ROI). Data science generates ROI when it informs resource allocations, investment decisions, or drives change in an organization or market. If the tools of data science are not focused on key behaviors, the project runs the risk of becoming a research initiative—great for some use cases, but not for putting insights into practice and generating ROI. Bringing in behavioral scientists to data science projects can provide insight into drivers and barriers of those key behaviors.

Behavioral scientists focus the team on the behavior to be influenced; starting with a decision or choice at the core of the behavior and working through the environmental elements that will move people towards or away from that behavior. Orienting teams on decisions immediately lines up the experts around the outcome of interest and the design of interventions to influence that outcome.

In the simplest terms, data scientists are hired for their ability to describe patterns in existing data and to generate predictive models that tell business leaders what's likely to happen in the future. Behavioral scientists are hired to generate hypotheses about why business metrics are what they are (based on the behaviors of employees or customers), and to design interventions to change behaviors—thus improving business metrics. When the two work together, they can offer insights and perspectives that lead to better business outcomes.

The best way for data scientists to begin to understand and describe patterns in current data is through unsupervised analyses—a type of exploratory analysis on a dataset with no pre-existing labels and limited pre-defined business rules. A behavioral scientist can support by analyzing the behavior and choices to glean insight (often segmented) for intervention design work. This is an important first step to avoid forcing your pre-existing mental models on the data. "Allowing the data to speak" without pre-defined business rules will generate ideas for interventions and more personalized nudges. You can still design interventions for a "To Be" future, but design work should start with "As Is" understanding of the choice environments that exist today, and the way it naturally (unsupervised) separates in data.

The data scientist can also work with the behavioral scientist on supervised analyses—a type of analysis that works towards a prediction (a target). Use the outcome of interest (the behavior or choice) as a target variable, making the goal of a model an outcome rather than just a risk prediction. Outcome, choice, and decision target variables also tend to lead analysts towards causal versus correlative insights. As an example from the medication adherence space, models of medication discontinuation become less about who will discontinue (and when), and more about predicting who is likely to respond to interventions, how, and when the offers will be most effective.

Data and behavioral scientists can work well together to answer the following questions that will organize teams around outcomes:

- What is the behavior we are trying to effect? (e.g. medication adherence)
- Where / when is a decision made that we can influence? (e.g. Rx refill)
- What is the cost of bad decisions? What is the benefit of a good decision?
- What are the individual, social, and/or environmental barriers to the right decision? (these can become predictors in a model!)
- What is the baseline effectiveness of interventions addressing those barriers today?
- What are the opportunities to re-define, re-prioritize, and personalize to address barriers and generate expected behavioral response?
- What is the cost of interventions we might define, and where is the highest return on interventions with similar cost profiles?
- How can we set up an experiment to evaluate success and improve future models?

Behavioral scientists will help to focus the team on the

behavior to be influenced; starting with a decision or choice at the core of the behavior and working through the environmental elements that will move people towards or away from that behavior. organizing teams around behaviors, decisions, and choices, data science insights will have clearer line of sight to the benefits of interventions. There is also an easier transition from design to experimentation, and eventually implementation phases when we keep the outcome measure in sight from the beginning. In the example of medication discontinuation, study how to improve refill rates vs. who is likely to discontinue—this small change will have an outsized benefit on behavioral insights teams.

How To Integrate Behavioral Science

Data science projects need behavioral scientists to avoid generating insights that are interesting, but then put on a shelf because they don't establish a clear link to actions that alter behavior and increase ROI. Insights extracted from data are powerful when coupled with a behavioral scientist working to define interventions and influence behavior. Data scientists can also benefit from insights that behavioral scientists can share based on research in areas like psychology and economics, such as the science of incentives and habit formation, especially as it relates to reinforcement learning (RL) projects. Working with behavioral scientists, RL projects can result in personalized nudges with personalized cues, recommended actions, and rewards. Behavioral scientists can also benefit from the insights of data scientists. Data science can help to optimize the treatment, tenor, and timing of behavioral interventions—analogous to the "4P" marketing analytics focus on product, place, promotion, and price (i.e. incentives). Data science can also be used to identify barriers in behavioral pathways to be removed so that a simple nudge can work. To build sustained behaviors and habits, insights on pathways and the "time phasing" of multiple actions and choices are important. Making the right choice the easy choice often has a temporal aspect where data science can help.

After using insight from data to design behavioral interventions, measurement of intervention effectiveness can benefit from a close partnership between behavioral and data scientists. Propensity scoring and "matched pair" analyses are important inputs to controlled experimentation—by getting experiments set up for success and also allowing for quasi-experimental methods that are useful when controlled experiment isn't feasible. In evaluating experimental results, sub-segmenting mining for differential response is a role the data scientist can play to inform potentially more targeted implementations.

Projecting experimental results and survey data to larger populations is yet another role for data science; as is finding proxy measures for intervention response. This is especially important when "fail fast" isn't an option, or when the outcome of measure is difficult to capture and proxy measures could be more accurate. Data science can therefore be a bridge between measurement programs and implementation of findings.

The Limitations Of Behavioral Science

A number of limitations are important to keep in mind while working to connect data and behavioral science. These limitations range from technical to theoretical, cultural, and ethical considerations when applying data-based insights to behavioral science

Most data science efforts glean insight from historical data and are limited by the range of experience that is available in historical data. Designing behavioral interventions solely on historical insight is like driving a car looking only in the rear view mirror. Complement historical data analysis with analogue-based analyses and focus groups. This will expand insight into areas not available in historical data and into areas that focus groups can extrapolate our thinking into new areas. Behavioral scientists will push the thinking of data scientists to look beyond the historical data—or at least put historical data in context of what can be learned about behavior in the past when designing for the future.

Data are also biased to the way and context with which they are collected. Predictive models have the potential to generate insights and recommendations that only confirm bias as opposed to generating actionable insight. Consider the bias in data, and develop and operate algorithms within a strict and formal ethical framework. Ask your teams about fairness, explanatory power, and robustness of model use:

- Fairness
  - o Does the algorithm display bias towards certain groups?
  - o Is any differential treatment of groups justified by underlying factors or is it avoidable?
  - o Are data used to build the model a fair representation of relevant populations?
  - o What biases exist in the underlying data and how it is collected?
- Explanatory Power
  - o What are the main contributors that influence the model output?
  - o How does each input factor influence the result?
- Robustness

o Will the model remain stable in the future and generalize well to unseen data?
o Is there a risk of bias appearing in the future as the model receives new data?

Additionally, recognize that most data are governed for certain uses and that data security and use considerations must be understood before undertaking an analytical effort. Beyond legal and regulatory risk considerations, consider reputational risk when adding data science to behavioral insights projects.

Expect counterintuitive insights and unexpected recommendations to be challenged by stakeholders who will want to hold onto their existing mental models. Fair or not, the reality is that data-driven insights are not always easy to adopt—at least not the ones that force a change in thinking. Plan for this change management time, and as you get closer to implementation, plan for the effort needed to change culture as reinforcement learning and applications driven by data and behavioral science personalize experiences beyond the existing simplified, segmented view of the world.

Consulting

Zarak Khan

Behavioral science can be used to strengthen and improve a variety of Practice Areas across an organization. Zarak Khan explains its application to Consulting.

How A Behavioral Scientist Contributes

Consulting at its core is about problem solving, which is a natural partnership for the tools of behavioral science. Perhaps this is why so many of the organizations identified in our survey are themselves consultancies. A behavioral scientist can augment an organization's consulting arm in a variety of ways, including:

- Providing a behavioral framework for understanding a problem and designing a solution
- Defining a problem from a behavioral perspective
- Assessing the impact of solutions

PROVIDING A BEHAVIORAL FRAMEWORK

Consultancies will all have process maps for how they solve a client's problems. These are step-by-step guides that, with some variation or nuances, generally follow the same steps: problem definition, solution generation, implementation, and monitoring or assessment. A behavioral scientist may add a few steps or complementary methodologies here, such as developing a behavioral map of key actions, barriers, and benefits.

Every consultancy will also have frameworks for problem-solving. It's kind of their bread and butter, and such frameworks are often considered some form of intellectual property. The best of these are easy to understand and can help a consultant walk a client through a problem and start to generate potential solutions. Behavioral scientists have their own frameworks that describe and predict human behavior. Some of the more well-known frameworks in behavioral science include:

- The EAST Framework—developed by the Behavioral Insights Team, it stands for "Easy, Attractive, Social, Timely" and is a simple way to assess and brainstorm interventions.
- The Fogg Model—created by Stanford professor BJ Fogg, this is a behavioral model that focuses on three elements for behavior: motivation, ability, and prompts.
- The Hooked Model—developed and popularized by Nir Eyal in his book *Hooked*. This model relates to the trigger, action, reward, and investment required to build and sustain a habit.
- The 3B Framework—created by Irrational Labs to apply behavioral science to design and strategy by focusing on behaviors, barriers, and benefits.
- And there are many more!

Frameworks are not universal. The relevant skill is knowing which framework to apply in which situation, and more importantly: how to create your own behavioral framework for a specific client or industry problem. This is harder than it sounds, as it requires deep knowledge of fundamental behavioral research as well as industry experience. Moreover, a weak framework can reveal a lack of knowledge in one or both of those areas.

DEFINING THE PROBLEM

Adding a behavioral scientist to your diagnosis phase should lead to a more comprehensive understanding of the problem you are trying to solve. A behavioral scientist accomplishes this in a variety of ways:

- Framing problems as a set of key behaviors that can be influenced
- Going beyond surveys and focus groups to review behavioral and administrative data that can show a person's true preference or action, not just their stated preference
- A greater emphasis on design and incentives within a system, as opposed to a focus on independent decisions.

It is difficult to overstate the importance of accurately diagnosing the problem you're working on. As Albert Einstein said, "If I had an hour to solve a problem, I'd spend 55 minutes thinking about the problem and 5 minutes thinking about solutions." Augmenting your standard set of diagnosis tools with a behavioral approach can ensure that your solutions are a better match to the actual problem at hand.

ASSESSING THE IMPACT OF SOLUTIONS

They may also contribute to a more robust assessment phase.

Many consulting projects only conduct a rudimentary pre/post implementation analysis and don't establish a causal relationship between their solution and what happens afterwards. It's worth noting that in many cases this may be due to a lack of interest on the part of the client to add elements to an assessment that add time and cost. Further, a consultancy is often hired because of its expertise, and it can be a bit of a tightrope to demonstrate expertise but still insist on evaluation to make sure your ideas worked.

For a more in-depth exploration of assessing impact, and thinking of research decisions as strategic decisions, check out the chapter on Research Methods in Business.

How To Integrate Behavioral Science

A consultancy of any size will already likely be a highly-matrixed organization that is adept at pulling in specialized expertise based on project need. If building a practice in behavioral science, it's advisable to start by hiring a senior behavioral scientist with both technical knowledge and business acumen. From there, you can hire mid-level and junior behavioral scientists to build out your delivery team. With the growth of the field and increase in formal, credible applied behavioral science education programs, it is becoming easier for organizations to hire talented young behavioral scientists into roles where they can grow and gain additional practical experience.

For most consulting teams, a behavioral scientist will join to augment the current efforts. As such, they might work alongside project managers, data analysts, and other consultants to improve the final deliverable.

If your organization is looking to more fully integrate behavioral science into its consulting effort, you might have a behavioral scientist review your current application and solution frameworks. This is often a fruitful first step because so much of the nature and process of the work stems from these documents. It may also help you integrate behavioral science if you think of the core of your work as behavior change. That simple shift can realign the way you approach projects and staff teams.

Behavioral scientists can be valuable in client-facing interactions as they can help articulate the behaviors that underlie clients' initiatives, and can lend credibility to the suggested approach.

The Limitations Of Behavioral Science

The main limitation of behavioral science here is tied to the broader limitations of consulting. Namely, you have limited control over the scope of your projects and the implementation of your recommendations.

It may also be challenging to delineate the responsibilities of a behavioral scientist relative to team members in communications, design, change management and other complementary roles.

A common point of failure is calling in a behavioral scientist towards the conclusion of a project and asking for input. Without the opportunity for that input to be incorporated in a meaningful way, behavioral science can become little more than window dressing to a product that has already been finalized. Incorporating behavioral science into the early discovery phases (and even in business development, when the work is being scoped) provides the greatest opportunity for impact.

Another common pitfall is a lack of clarity on how a behavioral scientist contributes. To help alleviate any friction, your first behavioral hire—the senior behavioral scientist—should develop clear processes and tools for the behavioral science role, and identify where and how they participate in consulting engagements.

PART III

OPERATIONALIZING
BEHAVIORAL SCIENCE

Team Structure Intro

Types Of Behavioral Science Teams

There are three common models for integrating behavioral scientists into an organization. The "individual contributor" model involves hiring one expert in behavioral science who works across the business. In addition to an understanding of core behavioral science content (e.g., nudges, heuristics, and biases), this person may also have deep expertise across subject areas like psychology and economics, as well as expertise in measurement and the research process. "Doing" behavioral science well requires knowledge in all of those areas, so if the behavioral science team has an N of 1, that 1 must have this broad and valuable skill set.

Moreover, that person is often not simply a researcher, but a champion, ambassador, and translator for behavioral science. They often spend a significant amount of time and effort building momentum for the use of behavioral science within the organization. It may go without saying, but this type of individual is incredibly difficult to find.

The "centralized team" involves the traditional team approach: A group of people who have behavioral science expertise work together closely, with regular group meetings, shared goals, and often a shared physical work space. Individuals on the team may have great overlap in their training and skill sets, or there could be diversity in their professional backgrounds (e.g., UX vs. cognitive psychology vs. design thinking).

Finally, the "integrated model" is where behavioral scientists are embedded across the organization, working side by side with people in the business. Their role is to use behavioral science to improve the products or services their team is responsible for, and the behavioral scientist has (or develops) deep expertise in that specific business function. This could be marketing, product design, data science, or customer experience, just to name a few.

Which Is best?

The *individual contributor* model is generally used as a gateway towards building a larger behavioral science team. One person can influence a handful of business objectives, but it's difficult (if not impossible) to find someone who has deep knowledge of all areas of a business. And even if you're able to do so, they won't have enough time to dedicate themselves deeply to many initiatives at once. An individual contributor *may* work for small companies with limited behavioral science needs. It *may* also work when a company has a large support network elsewhere who are working on the same problems (e.g., data scientists, UX testers), so that the behavioral scientist can rely on them to supplement their own work. But this is rare, and even in such cases a single person would only have the bandwidth to be something of an internal consultant, not deeply involved in guiding a range of work. In the right context, an individual contributor may be able to influence the business in ways such as:

- Building awareness of behavioral science and advocating for its use
- Contributing significantly to a few key business teams / objectives
- Creating and socializing frameworks to guide the internal use of behavioral science.

They would have difficulty, however, doing the following:

- Scaling their work across the organization
- Having a major influence on strategy or execution across more than a few projects
- Identifying, designing, and advocating for behavioral science interventions and also testing their impact.
- Educating others on how to use behavioral science in their roles (unless that's their only function).

Because most organizations have needs that exceed the bandwidth of one individual, the centralized and integrated team approaches will be more successful in most cases. Simply put, more people equals a greater impact on the organization, and greater opportunity to build relationships with business partners that will be critical for your success. Compared to an individual, a team can also bring to bear a much broader set of skills, ideas, and perspectives on a business need. And there is the potential to place individuals in areas where they will have the most impact given their unique talents and experiences. This is why few organizations rely on an individual contributor for long. It's also why we decided not to devote a chapter to this model; we did not want to create the impression that it is equal—in general—in its efficacy to the two models.

So which of the two more expansive models works best? There are strengths and weaknesses to each. Which one is best for a particular organization depends on factors like organizational structure, the nature of the business, how they plan to use behavioral science, and the extent to which senior leaders require the team to clearly measure their ROI.

The following two chapters will discuss the strengths and weaknesses of each approach to provide some food for thought for leaders who wish to build out a behavioral science team.

The Centralized
Team Approach

Matthew Battersby

As the previous section indicated, an organization's behavioral science function can be configured in a number of ways. In this section, Matthew Battersby details the *centralized team* approach.

Introduction

A centralized behavioral science team typically sits separately from any other specific business unit or function. It has the remit to work on projects across the organization. Whilst a mature centralized team may have behavioral scientists embedded within certain business units, it is primarily a separately resourced team.

There are three key success factors for an in-house behavioral science team. The team must be able to

1. Identify the right problems to focus on
2. Develop and test new solutions
3. Fully implement a solution

Often, having a centralized behavioral science team is the best way to achieve these, but some potential drawbacks need to be acknowledged and overcome.

Identify The Right Problems To Focus On

The best behavioral science units are problem-solving teams. Their success or failure is dependent on identifying the right problems and the best problem-solving approach.

A key challenge is that virtually no one knows they have a behavioral science problem. Few people are clear on the type of challenge to which behavioral science can be best applied. Instead, people have marketing, human resources, sales, technology or operations problems. We may know behavioral science can provide an answer, but most people often do not, so they may not approach us.

When they do consider behavioral science, it is often when a policy, product or process is failing, and they are hoping some behavioral science magic will save the day. However, often the reason something is failing is because it contradicts key behavioral principles and therefore requires redesign rather than remedial action.

The key advantage of a central team is the ability to seek out the best problems to solve from anywhere across the business. The 'best' problems are ones where the root of the problem is a specific behavior that needs changing to achieve a clear business goal. There are an almost unlimited number of these problems and corresponding opportunities, as so many products, policies and processes are based on flawed assumptions about human behavior—on how we believe people should think and behave rather than how they really do think and behave.

To be successful, a central behavioral science team needs to think like a consultancy, building deep understanding of the goals, functions and capabilities within a business to source these opportunities. This understanding usually depends on building relationships over time with leaders and behavioral science advocates throughout different areas of an organization. Since centralized team members do not have a default seat at the table during team meetings and client presentations, they must earn an invitation by serving as stellar colleagues and demonstrating their value and their desire to help the business solve its most critical problems. In building a centralized team, strong academic and career credentials will help team members get a foot in the door with business leaders; high levels of competency and collegiality will help them develop the relationships needed to move behavioral science initiatives forward.

Develop And Test New Solutions

Once the key problems have been identified, the focus shifts to developing solutions. Applied behavioral science is still in its infancy, and it is a highly contextual endeavor—what works in one setting may not work in a similar setting. So it is rare to find an existing insight that can be applied to solving a problem without both adaptation and testing. A behavioral science team therefore needs the capability, resources and influence to test and learn.

Running experiments within an organization is often the best way to test insights and potential solutions. However, field experiments with internal or external clients can take time and are often influenced by factors outside the team's control. This is especially the case for businesses that are not direct-to-consumer, do not have strong digital and data functions or operate in heavily regulated industries. In these situations a behavioral science team needs a budget to run its own experiments and research. Where a central team sits within an organization is therefore very important. If the team does not sit within a central research or innovation function, it can be much harder to secure funding for research and experiments.

Many organizations expect behavioral scientists to tell them which approach is best based on our knowledge and experience, and they dislike the complexity and the perceived opportunity cost that comes with testing different ideas against one another. Behavioral science leaders must find ways to communicate the long-term business value of experimentation to business partners. This can be harder for leaders of centralized teams as they may be seen as outsiders who don't fully understand what is at stake, or who care more about the science than about the bottom line. Experimentation will be met with resistance, so behavioral science teams must also be prepared to assess the effects of their interventions via non-experimental methods such as quasi-experiments and pre-post comparisons.

Fully Implement A Solution

Ultimately, all commercial behavioral science teams will be judged on their business impact rather than their research impact. Business impact relies on a solution being fully delivered, implemented and adopted, and making this happen requires an additional set of skills. These skills can vary across solutions but often include copywriting, design, user experience (UX), project management and training.

Acquiring and applying these skills is often the biggest challenge for a centralized behavioral science team. Sitting outside of an operational function means the team may not have direct access to the talent and support needed for implementation. Success therefore requires establishing relationships and ways of working with other key functions within the business. Although this is the right approach, it can make it difficult to highlight the unique contributions and value of the behavioral science work. For this reason, a mature and well-established behavioral science team may also include delivery specialists.

Conclusion

A successful behavioral science team is part brain and part muscle. Its brain will seek out the best problems on which to apply behavioral science and use research and experimentation to solve them. Its muscle will implement these solutions effectively within an organization, turning insight into sustained action.

A centralized team is ideally positioned to deliver the brain role. It can work across the whole business and engage the senior levels to focus on problem solving rather than solution rescuing. However, to do this successfully, the team likely needs its own research and experimentation budget, or must sit within a centralized function where these budgets and expectations already exist. The most challenging role for the centralized team is having the muscle to turn insights into action.

The Integrated Model

Linnea Gandhi

B ehavioral science can be configured in a number of ways within an organization. In this section, Linnea Gandhi details the *integrated model* approach.

Introduction

As was described in the previous chapter, a centralized team consists of a group of behavioral scientists who work as a team to find and solve problems across all areas of an organization. Typically, they are housed in their own unit and act as a shared service. In contrast to this, the integrated model places one or more behavioral science experts into a larger team that is dedicated not to a functional skill set but to a product, policy, or outcome prioritized by the organization.

This might be a brand or product team, or even a set of complementary brands or products. In consumer goods, this might be a single brand of lotion or all skin care products; in financial services, this might be a savings app or all consumer-facing financial wellness products; in life sciences, this might be a single insulin brand or all diabetes therapies; and in retail, this might be an e-loyalty program or all of e-commerce. Internal functions might similarly integrate a behavioral individual or team dedicated to, for instance, performance evaluation, or all of talent management, or all of people operations. The defining attribute with this model is that the product, policy, or program comes first. The behavioral skill set—like any other skills set members bring to that team—is secondary, subordinate, and no more special than any other.

The Benefits Of Investing For The Long Run

Organizations who adopt an integrated approach are more likely to benefit from deeper insights, greater impact on KPIs, and long-term team sustainability, compared to having a centralized team and certainly compared to having no behavioral science expertise at all.

As was mentioned in a previous chapter, the value of a behavioral science team is determined by its business impact. When a behavioral expert or team is dedicated to your brand, product, or policy—rather than stretching themselves thin across diverse areas of the organization—they naturally have the bandwidth to go deeper. You aren't just left with a high-level list of potentially relevant psychology concepts. You're supported by a nuanced analysis of which concepts relate to which customers in which contexts, what pitfalls to avoid, and how to evaluate them. Plus, these insights are delivered with language and examples that are immediately and exclusively relevant to your product or policy. No translation required.

An integrated approach not only enables a more sophisticated, precise, and practical application of behavioral science, it also ensures this application is directly relevant to your KPIs. The best way to illustrate this benefit is in contrast to the centralized model. A centralized team will care about the KPIs of whatever product or policy group they're supporting. But this team will also care about utilization rates, number of experiments launched (regardless of where, regardless of outcome), and number of projects with high visibility to senior leadership—from where the team's funding often comes. In contrast, when these individuals are integrated into the product or policy team itself, the metrics they care about are entirely and exactly what the team cares about. They can't be successful by merely providing an entertaining workshop or an intriguing set of ideas that end up sitting on a shelf; they must put the hard, operational work into making an impact on your long-term KPIs.

Finally, given the collaborative, long-term setup, the integrated model is less likely to experience the "organ rejection" that centralized behavioral resources sometimes do. There is no special title, no special treatment, no special budget set aside to cover short-term services. The individual or individuals are just another key part of the team, like everybody else.

What about the benefits for the behavioral individuals engaged in this integrated model? Perhaps the biggest is that they get to see actual results! They're not only close to the decision-making, they're part of it. They don't need to sell themselves or your ideas, they already have a seat (or seats) at the table. And just like anyone else on the team, as they earn their teammates' trust, they can quickly earn the right to try more complex, innovative techniques.

The Risks Of Finding The Right Fit

For all its long-term benefits, the integrated model requires significant up-front investment to match the right talent to the right teams, and its success rests on retaining a few key individuals.

As with any new role, the fit needs to be just right. The product or policy team needs to be open to contributions from behavioral theory and methods, with a short list of project opportunities already lined up. In turn, the behavioral expert who is hired needs to have experience in relevant research areas and techniques. This may leave many organizations in an odd catch-22: They need to write a job description to bring in the right sort of expert, but they may lack the expertise or experience to predetermine what "right" is. Which domain of behavioral science makes most sense? Social psychology, cognitive psychology, behavioral economics, behavioral finance, judgment and decision making, consumer marketing? Must the expert have a PhD or Masters in the field to be credible, or would years of applied experience suffice? Do organizational dynamics require that expert to have a few years of industry experience, or at least worked in a non-academic setting? Would it be best to hire by promoting and training internally, or looking outside the organization?

Even if a fit is found, a further complication arises from the risk of turnover of key sponsors. What happens if a sponsor of this new expert rotates off the team? Does that sponsor bring the expert with them, leave them behind, or put them up for adoption by another product or policy group in the organization? This risk is especially acute early on in the onboarding and integration of a behavioral expert.

A smaller, but still salient downside, is the opportunity cost of foregoing a more centralized behavioral team model. Centralizing naturally provides greater institutional insights and synergies over time, which one expert on one team cannot hope to replicate. Also, it will almost always be the case that a (centralized) team of smart behavioral scientists with diverse views and backgrounds will produce more and better ideas than a single individual.

For the integrated behavioral experts, the downside of this model is the classic tradeoff of breadth for depth. The scope of work will be narrower, so the ability to diagnose and design a specific context for behavior change must be worth it. Passion for the product or policy, the customer base, or colleagues on the team, become more essential. Finally, such experts need to be willing to give up on being the special go-to "behavioral person" for the organization, in order to become an equal member of the core product or policy team.

A Strategy For Easing Into Integrated Behavioral Expertise

There are a couple of ways to set your organization down the path of this integrated model at a pace that's appropriate for you.

One approach is to start with a centralized behavioral consulting model, trying out behavioral applications across the organization without much discrimination. The team's long-term goal should then be to use its shorter-term engagements to search out viable product and policy areas where an integrated model could add the greatest value. After a few years of this exploration, the team should make a business case and a bet on where to invest, evolving itself from centralized to integrated. Some experts break off to join those designated products and policies, while a few may stay behind as a small core training task force or knowledge hub.

Alternatively, a core group of behavioral experts could rotate between a range of policy or product teams for 6 to 9-month terms, much like a post-MBA leadership rotation. The behavioral experts get to try out the teams, and vice versa, with the long-term intent to identify a solid match.

For many organizations, the path to value from behavioral science isn't forming a "Behavioral Team." It's finding behavioral teammates, to partner in building, developing, and testing the core products and policies serving customers and employees.

Improving Strategic Decisions

Nicole Grabel & Meghann Johnson

Decision-making processes are influenced by the sorts of cognitive, emotional, and social forces in which behavioral scientists have expertise. Because of this, behavioral scientists are often asked to provide advice on strategic decisions made within an organization. Nicole Grabel and Meghann Johnson explain how behavioral science can guide and improve the strategic decision-making process.

Introduction

The next time your organization needs to make a strategic decision, learnings from behavioral science can help you avoid common pitfalls that tend to plague decision makers. This article suggests four broad focus areas for organizations, with potential biases and processes to improve their decision making in each:

1. Align on objectives.
2. Ensure all voices are heard and acknowledged.
3. Mitigate common biases in evaluation.

4. Thoroughly consider potential obstacles.

The processes that are suggested for avoiding or mitigating challenges around strategic decision making are based on behavioral science research. They are intended to give you a sample of the types of contributions a behavioral scientist would make to the strategic decision-making process, rather than to be an exhaustive description of how they may contribute.

Align On Objectives

The way the decision-making process starts sets the stage for the way the rest unfolds. One underestimated hurdle early on in strategic decision-making is aligning the team on the objective of the decision. Business decisions typically involve multiple stakeholders, each of whom may come in with different information and agendas. Though the decision they have to make—whether or not to move forward with a new product launch, how to structure sales incentives, or setting the right pricing strategy, for example—may seem to have a clear objective, a group of seemingly aligned decision makers may all be optimizing for different outcomes.

Take the decision of whether or not to launch a new product. A team would likely all align on the idea that the objective of the meeting is figuring out if it's best for the company to make the new product. But each person may have different ways of (implicitly) defining what that objective is. In the same group, one person may think about the "right" decision in terms of short-term sales performance, another in terms of long-term competitive position in the market, and a third by a measure of interpersonal success, like making the boss happy. The team should make explicit who or what would determine a good decision. Once the team has a discussion about the underlying objectives, they can better understand how to weigh the different aspects, and get everyone on the same page about the purpose of the decision. As obvious as it may seem, the first step of a good decision is aligning on what you're trying to accomplish by making the decision.

Ensure All Voices Are Heard And Acknowledged

The above assumes that the decision-making process will be undertaken by a team, not an individual. Of course, this is often the case, and certainly has the potential to lead to better decisions than leaving it to just one person. However, group dynamics are incredibly complex, and if they're not consciously accounted for, the decision outcome might be no better, and perhaps even worse, than if the decision had been left up to one person. For example, one issue seen time and again in groups ranging from classes to boardrooms is unequal participation. When certain members of the group consistently remain silent, the group doesn't reap the benefits of everyone's experience and perspectives.

People are especially likely to withhold their views if they perceive that they are in the minority. They might be worried about the social ramifications—and justifiably so. Social psychological research shows that when the majority of people in a group have a shared view, and one person holds another view, the group concentrates their collective social pressure on the holdout and judges him negatively if he does not change his mind (Wesselmann et al., 2014).[16] Traditional power dynamics can also play a role; if people who are well liked or who hold

---

16 Wesselmann, E. D. et al. (2014). "Revisiting Schacter's research on rejection, deviance, and communication (1951)". Social Psychology. 45: 164-169.

positions of power offer their opinion early on, this will almost certainly sway others in favor of that view and increase pressure to go along with it. People also may not speak up if they take the discrepancy between their perspective and others' as evidence that their view is wrong. This is known as informational social influence: the less sure we are about something, the more we look to others' opinions as evidence of what the right answer is.

Furthermore, even if everyone offers their perspective, some views might be weighted disproportionately more than they should be. For example, the confidence heuristic refers to our tendency to be more persuaded by people who present with more confidence. While sometimes confidence can be a signal of knowledge, that is, of course, not always the case, and can instead lead people down a false path.

One strategy to overcome these errors that can befall groups is gathering independent, anonymous assessments prior the group discussion. Keeping them anonymous helps everyone feel more comfortable offering their true view, using the information that they have. Collecting thoughts from everyone, and not just those who elect to speak up, helps ensure no voice falls through the cracks. This can allow for the group's collective intelligence to be harnessed more effectively.

Leaders can also play a critical role in how the group discussion unfolds and in ensuring that no view gets forgotten or discounted. A leader who actively encourages and shows appreciation for dissent, and even advocates for minority views that she may or may not actually hold, can help foster an open discussion and mitigate the tendency to conform to authority or majority opinion. Some leaders assign themselves or others to the role of "devil's advocate" to make it socially acceptable— even desirable—to highlight potential problems with a chosen course of action before it's too late.

Mitigate Common Biases In Evaluation

As the discussion progresses, there are many ways that irrelevant factors and biases can affect the judgment of each individual. For example, suppose you have already spent months developing the package design for a new product the team is deciding whether to launch. The sunk cost fallacy might compel you to want to move forward with the product launch so it doesn't feel like all that work went to waste—even though you might be increasing inefficiencies further by putting more resources behind a product it would be unwise to launch. Take another example: consider if another company recently had a lot of trouble launching a similar product. The availability bias, which refers to our tendency to overweigh the probability of events that easily come to mind, might cause us to firmly believe the launch isn't a good idea, regardless of more evidence suggesting it would be. Confirmation bias—the tendency for us to seek out and pay more attention to information that supports what we already believe—could cause an opposite effect. We might dismiss (or not even notice to begin with) important evidence suggesting that we should pause and revise our plan.

Because behavioral scientists are aware of these biases, they can help you create processes to avoid them. They may, for example, suggest developing standard assessment criteria in advance of the decision-making process. This can ensure that team members are thinking specifically and deliberately about how the choice performs on important attributes. By starting by judging the different choices on the criteria devised, rather than a "gut" or "overall" feeling, this can keep biases that might more strongly come into play when assessing decisions more holistically in check.

Thoroughly Consider Potential Obstacles

Finally, as groups draw nearer to coming to a decision, it is natural that they might focus more on the reasons a likely path is a good one, and overlook potential obstacles that could arise. To ensure weaknesses in a plan are given serious consideration, a behavioral scientist may suggest a 'premortem'.[17] A premortem is just like a post-mortem evaluation, but it is before a decision is made. The team imagines that the decision is made and something has gone wrong, and each member lists potential reasons for the failure. This can help ensure it's not just an idealized, theoretical version of an idea that's being decided on—rather, potential glitches that might typically only be obvious once the project is underway can be realized earlier. This also creates another space (in addition to the earlier devil's advocate strategy) for people who might have had concerns, but felt uncomfortable saying so, to state them in a more sanctioned way. Because new information is gathered over time, it's important to create standard processes that encourage people to express doubts or concerns at multiple points.

Limitations

While these strategies have been shown to help in decision making, it should be noted that they are certainly not foolproof. For example, if everyone in the group has a common bias or is exposed to the same misinformation, even the best decision-making hygiene will not be able to make up for that.

Additionally, it's important to keep in mind that making the best decision doesn't necessarily mean you'll achieve the

---

17 Klein, G. (2007). "Performing a Project Premortem". Harvard Business Review. 85 (9): 18–19.

best outcome. Inherent in most decision making is a level of uncertainty, and as long as some aspects of the outcome are unknowable ex ante, there is no way to guarantee a desirable result. These behaviorally-informed strategies, however, will allow you to be more mindful of social pressure and biases and more careful in your decision making.

Research In The Real World

Rachelle Martino

B ehavioral science can be used to strengthen and improve a variety of Practice Areas across an organization. Rachelle Martino explains how to liberate research from the lab and operationalize it within a real-world setting.

Reacquaint Yourself With The Scientific Method

In general—and especially in business settings—the title of 'Researcher' is uncommon, but chances are that research is a crucial component of your job. The goal of research is simple and profound: to systematically increase the stock of knowledge. If you work in a job that requires creative problem solving, or even if you advise individuals who do, you're probably conducting or at the very least making use of research. Every hiring or compensation plan you formulate, every time you assess a set of vendors with the goal of choosing the best one, and whenever you make updates to a process or website based on customer feedback, you are engaging in some type of research process.

The goal of research is to generate new knowledge, but to

complete research in this field is to commit to a process we're typically introduced to at a young age: the scientific method. Your current familiarity with this simple and profound procedure is probably directly correlated to the number of tri-fold foam display boards you've labored over, and in case the last and only time you've thought about the scientific method was during the 7th grade science fair unit here is a refresher:

1. Define purpose (identify a problem)
2. Construct hypothesis (clarify the problem)
3. Test the hypothesis and collect data (determine what data would help solve the problem)
4. Analyze data (organize the data)
5. Draw conclusions (interpret the results)
6. Communicate results

Middle school science teachers should feel fully vindicated, because in the future when their class asks, "When are ever going to use this?" at some inevitable low point in the school year, hopefully they know to retort, "Just you wait".

Conducting vs. Consuming Research

There is an argument that applying behavioral science should mean just that—applying the research that others have already investigated. After all, what is the point of learning all of the fascinating concepts and interventions that comprise the field we call Behavioral Science if you have to constantly do research to confirm that the idea does indeed work? Shouldn't the scientists have ironed out all the kinks and confusion when they were doing their research? Unfortunately, no.

For one thing, the context and environment you are working

in will be different from theirs, and this can have a massive impact on your results. As an example, much of behavioral science research is completed in a contrived setting. Undergrad students looking for a bit of extra credit are brought into a lab and sit at a computer where they are asked to weigh their preference for different priced items on a mocked-up retail website. How likely is it that the effect size observed by the lead researcher will be similar to what would be observed if that same intervention were pushed live onto Ali Express's online marketplace? Not very.

Additionally, every research finding has boundary conditions. Often we find that an effect holds only under some circumstances. As an example, do people learn better when they study in silence or with some noise? A classic study found that introverts do better when they study in silence, while extraverts do better when they studied with music on. It can take dozens if not hundreds of studies to fully understand the boundaries of a particular effect.

All that being said, utilizing what others have found through past research is sometimes the best or only source of confidence in the application. Often we can't conduct our own (especially experimental) research because

- It's not ethical. For example, it could involve a violation of people's privacy, or it could potentially result in harm (compared compared to baseline) for some participants. (refer to chapter on ethics). Example: We want to know whether a $10,000 bonus leads employees to be more productive than a $5,000 bonus. Assigning your employees to these conditions randomly does not seem fair to those in the $5,000 group.
- It's not possible. For example, if we want to know how being raised by a single parent impacts perseverance in

adulthood, we simply can't randomly assign people to either be raised by a single parent or not.

- It's not practical. This can be for a variety of reasons. A common one is that the insights gained from the experiment really can't be scaled up in a meaningful way (E.g., does giving people a sabbatical increase retention?). Another common reason is that the insight that would be gained by the research does not justify the expense of conducting it. Even if you find what you expect, it does not pass the "so what?" test.

In most situations, the best result will be a product of both consuming past research, and conducting additional research that is specific to your application area and objectives. Weighing existing research is an excellent tool to generate and prioritize ideas, get inspired by the methods and approaches that have been used in the past, and to calibrate confidence in your own future research strategy.

How To Conduct Research

In general, behavioral scientists are hired to test and demonstrate causal relationships—that changing something (e.g., reducing the price) will lead to a behavioral change of some sort (more sales). The success of your business research efforts, however, will depend on how well you can define your research purpose and objectives. Before you start collecting data or looking for research that has already been published, you should be able to clearly and succinctly articulate the question you are asking. There are three main types of questions you may seek to answer on the journey from exploration to explanation.

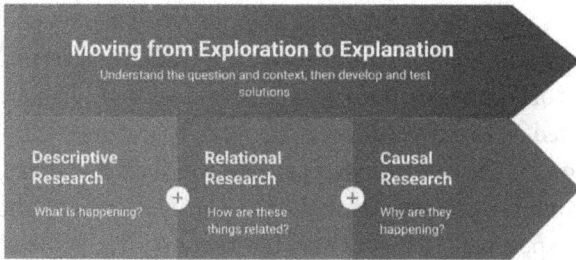

Moving from Exploration to Explanation
Understand the question and context, then develop and test solutions

Descriptive Research	Relational Research	Causal Research
What is happening?	How are these things related?	Why are they happening?

Descriptive research: Studies designed primarily to describe what is going on or what exists.

- In product design: What is the typical user flow through our new app?
- In retail: What is the average "basket" for a single purchase?
- In healthcare: What % of our patients have been vaccinated?
- **What is happening?**

Relational research: Studies designed to look at the relationships between two or more variables.

- In product design: Does app usage in the first week after download predict whether people will still be using it a year later?
- In retail: Do people who use coupons have smaller or larger "baskets" than those who don't?
- In healthcare: Is there a relationship between geographic region and willingness to be vaccinated?
- **How are these things related?**

Descriptive and relational research primarily help us to understand the world as it is before we intervene to try to change it. Many of us, however, are hired to determine the kinds of language, products, and processes that can be reliably counted on to drive a desired *change* in behaviors and business outcomes. This requires that we conduct causal research. Causal research is synonymous with the term "experiment" because only experimental designs have the necessary features to identify causal relationships.

Causal research: Studies that tell us whether changing one thing causes a change in another thing.

- In product design: Does switching from points to badges *increase* sales productivity?
- In retail: Does soft music or upbeat music in a retail store lead to *more* sales?
- In healthcare: Does an automated daily reminder from a loved one *increase* medication compliance?
- **Does this intervention lead to an *improvement in* that outcome?**

The best way to determine what research approach to use is to thoroughly understand the problem you are trying to address. In a business setting, it can be easy to put the cart before the horse and try to jump into experimentation without fully understanding the problem space or defining the objectives. Experiments also typically require more resources than the other kinds of research. This is why—in general- it's prudent to explore your variables of interest (descriptive research) and learn how different variables are related to one another (relational research) before investing in an experiment.

SIGNS THAT YOU'RE STILL EXPLORING

- You're not exactly sure you're even asking the right question yet
- You're trying to generate a bunch of ideas for a given goal but you have no method or ability to prioritize them yet
- You don't know what level of detail or 'unit' your research should be on
- You can get at least part way to the answer you want by looking for what others have done
- You don't exactly know what you want to do with this information so you allow things to be flexible until after you start getting your arms around the problem

If you are in this space, push on stakeholders to get to an appropriate level of detail required to write a hypothesis. It's critical to determine what type of research question you have, so that you can select the method that will best (and most efficiently) answer it.

SIGNS THAT YOU'RE READY TO EXPERIMENT

- You're prepared to select across one of several options if only you knew which is best
- You have a clear north star objective and way of assessing what is 'best'
- You have a data-backed hunch about what idea best answers your research objective but you need to know for certain before moving forward
- Experimenting in the way you're planning is ethical, possible, and practical

If you are in this space, you are ready to design an experiment that can help you answer a causal research question.

Tools In Your Toolkit

In the previous section, we looked at nuances around the type of research question you're asking. Here, we look at different kinds of data we can collect to answer that question. Different sources and types of data have different strengths and weaknesses, and lend themselves more readily to the three different kinds of research questions (descriptive, relational, and causal). You'll notice that the methods for capturing data that are the most convenient for researchers and the least invasive for participants (described first in our list) yield rather limited insights. In general, the more deeply we engage with participants directly, the more opportunity there is to learn.

SECONDARY DATA ANALYSIS

Modern businesses are continuously investing in their data collection and analytics capabilities. With every program and process that passively codifies aspects of a business's operations, sales, finance, marketing, hiring, or training in a structured data format there is an opportunity to regress, track, summarize, correlate, conduct unsupervised learning, and ultimately synthesize answers to a great many research questions. Enterprise data warehouses, google analytics, and publicly available data sets can provide a great deal of insight into customer behavior.

> **Good for:** Research questions that can be answered with naturally occurring data that is available to you. You can answer descriptive questions and you can run statistical analyses to help answer relational questions.

Bad if: you have no access to relevant secondary data, or if you want to study mindsets, opinions, values and other items that are not directly observable. Because you can't experiment on secondary data sets, you can't answer causal questions with much certainty. Also, if the quality of the data are poor, you may be better off with no data at all.

NATURALISTIC OBSERVATION

Here, we learn about behaviors from watching research subjects in their natural environment, so long as it's socially, legally, and ethically acceptable to do so. The key factor is that they don't know you're watching and you don't interfere, you simply observe.

Good for: Observing and describing common behaviors that are exhibited in a public setting. Especially useful if people are unwilling or unable to describe their behavior with accuracy if you were to ask them after the fact. For instance, people might self-report wiping down exercise equipment after each use, but their actions might tell a different story.

Bad if: You're studying things that can't be publicly observed via behavior, such as attitudes or emotions; you want to know *why* people are doing what they do, as opposed to just what they're doing (i.e., you can't answer causal questions).

SURVEYS, FOCUS GROUPS AND INTERVIEWS

Surveys ask the same questions to a large number of partici- pants. We use their answers to describe their opinions, attitudes, behaviors, or experiences. Likert scales (strongly disagree— strongly agree) are generally used to capture intensity of attitude or preference. Participants can offer numerical estimates of behaviors like spending or sleep. And free-form text fields can be used to explore beliefs, values, or detailed evaluations. This is an incredibly versatile data collection strategy that can be used to explore topics of interest, investigate possible relationships between variables, and keep a pulse on changes over time.

Interviews are similar to questionnaires, but the interviewer usually works with a smaller number of participants in a deeper, more qualitative way. Often these supplement survey data. For example, you might deploy a large survey to gauge consumers' attitudes towards new product options, then conduct lengthy interviews to find out why they have those preferences and how you could create the optimal price/feature mix.

> **Good for:** If you are interested in both learning about behavior and getting at some of the 'why' behind what might be driving it. Primarily used for descriptive and relational research questions.

> **Bad if:** You're studying things that people can't articulate consciously. For example, if asked why they chose the cell phone they have, most people would offer several reasons, but there are many factors that influenced them outside of their conscious awareness (e.g., the friendliness or pushiness of the clerk, how competing phones were priced and organized to lead you to a particular one). Self-report tools are prone to several kinds of bias such as social desirability (wanting to look or feel good) and demand characteristics (telling you what you want to hear). It can also be challenging to get a representative sample when people can willingly opt in or out of participation, as often only those with extreme views take the time to speak up.

USABILITY TESTING

Making time and opportunity for naive users to try and navigate a new website or app while designers or researchers prompt or at least watch is a humbling and important part of any product development process. Usability testing is helpful in many stages of product design, including workshopping new ideas for emotional pull or usability, improving flow or simplicity, and checking finished products for red flags before they roll out to a broad audience.

> **Good for:** Pilot testing new ideas or product features to identify the most effective one, working out the kinks or red flags in new product offerings, websites, advertisements before they are made public.

> **Bad if:** You're not sure what the key things are to test or how to improve them; you test so late in the process that your results can't be incorporated into future strategy.

EXPERIMENTATION

Experimentation is most clearly delineated by the testing of hypotheses to try and learn about cause and effect relationships. This is the most rigorous method, and the only one that can definitely answer the question of whether changing one thing *causes* a change in something else. There are three fundamental ingredients in a true experiment:

1. Identification and measurement of a key outcome. This is called the "dependent variable" and might be something like *sales*. This outcome is measured for every participant across the experiment.

2. A change or intervention introduced by the researcher. This is called the "independent variable" and might be something like *offering a coupon*. In the experiment, we're testing whether receiving the intervention changes

scores on our dependent variable. In this example, we'd test whether *receiving a coupon* increases *sales.*

3. Random assignment of people to at least two groups to compare to each other. In the simplest case, we have a group who got the coupon called the treatment group—and a group that did not—called the control group. This ensures that the only thing that differs between the groups is that one group got our intervention (coupon) and the other did not.

To be clear, the dependent variable is the thing we're interested in increasing or decreasing (e.g., sales) and the independent variable is our idea of how to do so (e.g., a coupon). Inexperienced researchers often lead their study design by identifying an intervention they're interested in and designing an experiment to find out "what happens" if people receive the intervention. The most impactful research almost always flows in the other direction: Identify the business outcomes that most need to improve (your dependent variables) and then design interventions (independent variables).

While we suggest creating a hypothesis in order to define an experimental research question, it is not a requirement. There is a possibly apocryphal story about Google testing forty-one different shades of blue on a webpage to see which would result in the best business performance. No person in their right mind could have hoped to offer a hypothesis about which color would win before testing, but that didn't mean that the 'winning' shade didn't truly outperform the others. As few companies have the resources and ability to run thousands of tests per year on every aspect of participant experience, a carefully informed hypothesis helps to focus scarce resources on the ideas that are most likely to work, and to influence the most important outcomes.

As the experimental process expands from the University

lab to the rest of the world, it's useful to distinguish between subcategories of experiments.

Field experiments

A field experiment involves changing something the direct experience of your treatment group and observing the impact on a "real life behavior" you care about. Executing experiments in real-life scenarios is fascinating and incredibly challenging. Some of the key things to consider are the ethics of manipulating your independent variable, the validity of your dependent variable measurement, and the generalizability of your findings to participants and situations outside of your testing situation. An undergraduate level research methods book can be a great resource for learning more.

In-person, field experiments are commonly executed in 'blocked' designs. Instead of trying to randomly augment half of the customers' experience that walk through the door, it is simpler to implement an intervention at a *store* level. For example, a chain of hair salons may decide that for a period of time a random selection of 'x' salons will try implementing strategy 'x' while the remaining (still random) selection of 'y' salons will try implementing strategy 'y'. Blocked designs generally lack the statistical power of traditional experiments, and they're not as robust for identifying causality. But they are better than non-experimental designs for testing causal relationships.

Digital A/B tests

Digital A/B tests are online experiments that are usually done to test how changing something in a person's digital experience impacts later behavior. As an example, participants go to book a room through a travel site. Unbeknownst to them, half of them see a version of the page with a family canoeing (version A) and the other half see a big city skyline (version B). The company is testing which of these leads to more bookings, and tomorrow they will implement the winner as their cover page. Companies like Google and Facebook have popularized the concept, and if you interact with any web page, app, or corporate marketing campaign, it's likely that what you're seeing is the end result of dozens to thousands of A/B tests. Digital spaces have become popular 'labs' for experiments because enabling technology can code A/B tests right into the interfaces that customers interact with, and the dependent variable metrics we're influencing are usually already being measured.

Lab experiments

There are many situations where running a field experiment is impossible. A single site restaurant that wants to try out a new menu pricing scheme to see if it will increase average order values, for example. Since it may be impossible to A/B test prices without risking serious reputational injury, an experiment designed into a simulated environment may suffice. Individuals fitting the average customer profile can be invited to individually view one of two menus with different pricing variants and provide their anticipated order value if they were to receive such a menu in a restaurant on an online platform like Amazon's Mechanical Turk. We can't be sure that what we learn in this context will absolutely translate to the business setting and hold true over time. But some information is better than no information at all, and lab studies are often quick and inexpensive ways to get a general pulse check on an idea.

> **Good for:** Getting at true causal relationships. Think of this as clinical research for business. You take Advil and your headache goes away. Someone studied it, proved it worked, and then it was rolled out broadly to consumers. If you want to

know whether changing or investing in a new approach yields dividends that would justify it, you want to run an experiment.

Bad if: You don't have the expertise or resources to design and interpret high quality experiments. If you don't have access to participants who are representative of your sample (whatever you find won't necessarily carry over to the situations you care about). Also if you're studying something that can't be truly randomly assigned* because of ethical or practical reasons.

*Quasi-experiments

Often a researcher cannot randomly assign subjects to a treatment vs. control group because it is not feasible or ethical. A grocer can't randomly assign individual participants to either a calm music vs. upbeat music condition because there's only one sound system in the store. So they might opt to play the soft music for a week, then the upbeat music the next week, and compare sales. The problem here is that other things may have differed besides the music. One week might have been closer to a holiday, or they could have better sale prices one week vs. the other. These become alternative reasons why sales could have been better (in research these are called *confounding variables*). True experiments eliminate confounding variables by ensuring that participants experience the exact same thing at the exact same time, except for the different music. Quasi-experiments can be thought of as a next-best-thing when experiments are not possible and are often conducted in close partnership with a data science team.

Building A Research Presence

The benefits of doing research in business cannot be overstated.

Over the past five years, experimentation as a core business function has become more the norm than the exception at large tech- based companies precisely because they have come to understand the value of it. However, tech companies are at an advantage because of their innovative cultures and their ability to quickly A/B test most aspects of their business (e.g., landing pages, app features) with the click of a button, with thousands of built-in participants. They often have the benefit of being able to glance over and dismiss ethical and practical considerations as their tests generally involve changing images, text flow, and other things that users consider it the company's rightful purview to change.

Building out a research presence at other types of organizations may be more challenging. Field experiments involving employees and customers are generally more complex and sensitive than online A/B tests. A research practice will be most successful if it involves collaboration across the organization, both to produce better research and to garner organization-wide buy-in. An IT or data team may have knowledge of and access to data you'll need to understand how your key variables behave right now. Business leaders are best able to identify the key business challenges that need to be addressed, and metrics that need to be improved on. And data and behavioral scientists are most effective when they work together to blend experimental and non-experimental methods to gain a more complete understanding of what drives customer and employee behavior, and how we can change it.

Completing good business research often requires the team to slow down, invest more, think harder, and be more closely aligned. This is particularly true of experimental research that's meant to identify the best path forward. Just getting to the level of alignment required to formulate an adequately precise hypothesis is no easy task.

Because good research practices take time, resources, and focus—something that no business ever has enough of—here are some tips that may help with buy-in:

- Some people will understand the value and be excited about the idea of running experiments. Other people may find even that term intimidating. For those people, consider putting things in terms they already use, such as "pilot" or referring to it as measuring the impact or ROI. They may also respond more readily to an argument that highlights the risks of *not* conducting research (i.e. "We're about to invest a million dollars in this product—we should create a plan to make sure it's working.")

- Build engagement (and validation) by inviting your stakeholders to take part in prediction exercises before you begin your research. Documenting what everyone believed prior to the start of research makes it easy to highlight how much people have learned, and it is also a low-stakes way to keep interest levels high. It's like a raffle where first prize is the opportunity to tell everyone, "I knew it all along!".

- Try not to slow down or add too much complication to whatever process was typically used in the past. Doing so creates a heavier lift for you and creates more opportunity for unexpected things to go wrong.

- Weigh the need to learn against the need to improve mission-critical business outcomes. Make sure you are explicit about which avenue you are taking—not every project accomplishes both objectives.

- Prioritize. Not everything can be an experiment or a rigorous data collection exercise. Three weaker signals all pointing in the same direction (pre-post comparison, focus group conclusions, and survey-based indicators) may suffice when the stakes aren't that high.

In this chapter, we've introduced you to some of the considerations that come with conducting behavioral science research in an organizational setting. This is the metaphorical tip of the iceberg; there's a wealth of information not covered here. If you're new to experimentation, it's a good idea to hire someone who has experience with behavioral science in a business setting, and who has the perspective to understand how it should both stem from and inform other areas of the business. The more you dig into the topic the more you'll find that behavioral research is a fun way to cultivate your curiosity, partner with colleagues, and have a measurable impact on business strategy & outcomes.

Getting Started With
An Ethical Foundation

Scott Young

The previous chapters looked at some key elements of starting a behavioral science function in your organization. This chapter expands on how to get started and, crucially, how to place ethics at the center of your work. As behavioral science has made the jump to industry from academia, where research is governed by an Institutional Review Board, thoughtful practitioners seek guidance on how to ethically apply their knowledge. Scott Young offers some suggestions for how behavioral scientists should think about ethics in application and important questions to consider.

Introduction

Richard Thaler often signs copies of his landmark book "Nudge: Improving Decisions About Health, Wealth and Happiness" with the inscription and admonition to "Nudge for Good." He's also written frequently and passionately about the evils of "sludge" (using behavioral science principles in ways that ultimately harm people, or that run counter to their own well-being). His co-author Cass Sunstein, in turn, has written an entire book regarding the ethics of applied behavioral science.

Clearly, the pioneers of this revolution realized from the beginning that there were ethical issues associated with choice architecture and nudging behavior change. To put it another way, they recognized that behavioral science was a method—and it could be applied to either help people or confuse and deceive them. To their credit, they emphasized and illustrated positive, pro-social applications (smoking cessation, retirement savings, etc.), and continue to argue publicly against using behavioral science for nefarious ends.

As we turn to the private sector, these ethical questions take on additional dimensions. After all, most businesses are driven primarily by a profit motive. For the purposes of this conversation, we can assume that they are operating legally and serving an underlying need. However, that's not to say that there aren't many "shades of grey" involved. Nudging people to eat more chips may be good for a business, its employees and shareholders, but it's harder to argue that it is clearly good for society. Nudging salespeople to sell the most expensive and profitable products may drive revenue, but is it ethical?

This reality poses many challenging questions for private sector organisations, regarding the application of behavioral sciences:

- How can organizations apply behavioral science ethically in support of their profit motive?
- Should behavioral science be employed across all activities—or only within some functions?
- How and when is it ethical to nudge employees and customers?

Inevitably, organizations will have different approaches to these ethical questions. Some are already oriented towards business models that emphasize customer and employee retention, positive social impact and/or long-term profitability—and they will most likely view behavioral science through this lens. Others are arguably more transactional in nature and may think entirely in the context of ROI. This raises yet another question, as to whether or not it's possible to apply these tools ethically within an organisation that is pursuing questionable marketing or business practices.

We'd argue that employing these new tools and frameworks properly is vital to their internal acceptance and long-term effectiveness. Thus, applying behavioral science ethically is not only the right thing to do, it's also a good business strategy. To that end, let's briefly discuss three ways that leaders and internal champions can help ensure that their organisations are on the right track.

Define Behavioral Science For Your Organization

Perhaps a leader's most important role lies in effectively "defining" behavioral science within the organisation. How does it fit? What should it be used for? These questions have obvious practical implications, in terms of driving acceptance and setting realistic expectations.

To that end, an important starting point is to position behavioral science as a complement to existing efforts. It is a new, additional framework with which to view opportunities and challenges, through the "lens" of human heuristics and behavior change. Thus, it can potentially add value to nearly all aspects of an organisation, from insights to marketing and management. However, it is best viewed—and most likely to be embraced—as a "extra tool in the toolkit," rather than a replacement for tested approaches.

In parallel with "framing" and positioning behavioral science for internal adoption, there's the challenge of defining these tools from an ethical perspective. What are the standards for use? Who gets to decide?

In the absence of clear policies, guidelines or limits, it's quite likely that behavioral science will be applied to support or enhance anything that the organisation is doing today. Most likely, marketers and sales teams will naturally gravitate towards employing choice architecture, heuristics and nudges to drive revenue. For example, they may integrate defaults to "make it easier" for customers to automatically enroll or renew their purchases. Or they may add higher-priced options to influence choice architecture and subconsciously lead customers toward higher spending. And frankly, these approaches can easily be rationalized as simple extensions of current marketing efforts.

Thus, it is up to management to proactively address this issue, by outlining a philosophy underlying the use of behavioral science. Here, we can suggest emphasizing two ideas:

The objective of moving people from Intent to Action

The unique strength of behavioral science lies not in awareness or persuasion, but rather in helping those who are "already convinced" overcome their inertia and adopt new behaviors. In other words, it is best at facilitating change.

The pursuit of long-term customer and employee relationships

There's no question that these tools can be used to mislead people into splurging, super-sizing and spending more. But frequently, people will later regret these decisions and most likely resent (and possibly avoid) the organisation involved. Similarly, some employees will have concerns and qualms as well. Clearly, this is not a promising long-term business strategy.

It's far better to instead position behavioral science as a vehicle to help clients solve their larger life challenges (tied to health, wealth and happiness)—and/or for employees to "do the right thing" (tied to diversity, sustainability, etc.). In both cases, the potential rewards are significant. If an organisation can truly help a person solve a life challenge—or help an employee to feel good about herself and her company—they are likely to be rewarded with long-term loyalty.

Set The Tone By Starting Internally

A related question is where and how to begin applying behavioral science within an organization. On one level, this is a structural issue, which is addressed in greater depth elsewhere in this book. But it should also be considered from an ethical perspective, as the first projects can be powerful in setting a message across the organisation.

For this reason, we recommend starting your application of behavioral science Internally (among employees), rather than Externally (among customers). In fact, there are several benefits to beginning by nudging employee behavior, such as healthy eating, sustainability or diversity/inclusion.

- First, efforts among employees are inherently lower risk, from a revenue and business standpoint—and thus, a good "testing ground" for new tools and approaches.
- Second, they also tend to be quite salient and visible within the organisation, which can raise awareness, bring behavioral science "to life" and create success stories that resonate strongly.
- Third, you may have better existing data sources, and greater control over the data you can collect, for

employees. This can help you to understand the impact your interventions have on key outcomes before you extend them to customers.

- Fourth, these initiatives are very likely to steer the organisation in a positive ethical direction, as they don't raise the temptation (or accusation) of manipulation.

Of course, this is not to say that behavioral science can't be applied ethically in marketing, insights, CX, design and sales functions—and depending on the scope and mandate of your team, you may need to start directly with external-facing initiatives. Indeed, there are likely larger rewards, returns and ROI in these disciplines. However, as noted earlier, there are inherently greater challenges and risks as well, most notably balancing immediate financial incentives (to sell and profit) with ethical considerations (towards customers). Thus, organisations may be well-served to learn and "set precedent" internally, before moving on to external audiences.

Finding The Right Projects

Most likely, the selection and management of specific behavioral science projects will be delegated. However, organisational leaders can help shape and influence this process, by providing frameworks and criteria to help guide decision making. Here, we can offer three guidelines, particularly as efforts involve influencing external audiences (customers, guests, etc.)

BEGIN WITH THE BUSINESS CASE (AND EXISTING INTENT)

The reality is that in a business context, pilot projects are more likely to get funded (and later recognized) if their financial impact can be clearly and easily quantified. Thus, we do encourage clients to look for opportunities with clear, measurable ROI potential (most likely via cost savings or increased revenue). Behavioral science doesn't need to be limited to philanthropy and corporate social responsibility, as this limits its potential and undersells its impact. And pursuing positive ROI can be compatible with ethical considerations, provided that other important criteria are met.

For example, many hotel chains are losing millions in wasted food and energy use. This dollar figure helps frame (and justify) an investment in applying behavioral science to nudge guests in ways that could reduce this waste, much of which is inadvertent.

This final point (that the waste is inadvertent) is important, as nudging should not require convincing or coercing people, nor tricking them into new choices against their wishes. Instead, the goal is to help them convert their (positive) intent into action. In fact, if an effort requires helping people to act on their existing opinions/beliefs, it is likely a good fit for behavioral science tools.

DEFINE THE BEHAVIORAL CHANGE (ETHICALLY)

For many clients, the most challenging step is viewing and defining their challenges through a behavioral lens. Often, they start with very broad objectives, such as "get more people to use our product," and have difficulty articulating exactly which actions need to change. Yet the more narrowly managers can define desired changes (i.e., who does what differently), the more likely they are to succeed.

For an Italian digital payments company we worked with, ethnographic research revealed that the primary behavioral opportunity lay in moving people from cash to digital for their small, everyday transactions. This transition was not only a business opportunity for the company but also provided clear convenience and security for consumers. Ultimately, this led to specific nudges targeted to newsstand/kiosk environments, reminding customers of digital payment options and benefits at their point of decision.

Of course, this moment of definition also provides an opportunity to reconsider ethical dimensions. Is this specific behavior change in the best interest of the consumer? Is there evidence of incoming intent or openness to this change? Are we moving people from Intent to Action—or do they need to be actively persuaded or convinced?

FOCUS ON "WIN-WIN-WIN" OPPORTUNITIES

Finally, we encourage private sector clients to search for changes at the intersection of what's good for the company, its customers, and society. While this vision may sound idealistic or simplistic, it is actually a strong and realistic foundation for building long-term customer relationships. And importantly, there are clear opportunities across all business sectors:

- In financial services, businesses can better help investors to save money and plan properly.
- In health care, organizations can help ensure that patients take their medicines as directed.
- In hospitality, hotels can help guests conserve energy and reduce waste.
- In retail and consumer goods, marketers can help people select products that best fit their needs, objectives and budgets.

In our experience, it's important for organisations to aim for these positive, pro-social outcomes, with the understanding that "shades of grey" will emerge in implementation, as they consider specific behavior changes and interventions. For example, it can often be difficult to determine if a particular action is clearly in the customers' best interest—and in some cases, organisations may conclude that it is OK to "nudge for neutral," provided that they are not intentionally deceiving, nor clearly hurting customers.

Navigate The Grey Area With Tools And Processes

If efforts are guided and grounded by clear, positive objectives, it becomes easier to navigate these real-world ethical issues and challenges. In addition, it's valuable to provide business teams with processes and tools to help them evaluate new opportunities and/or proposed interventions.

For example, teams could be provided a set of questions to use in deciding whether to pursue a given project or effort, such as:

- Would you be comfortable with this intervention, if you or a family member were the customer or participant involved?
- Would you be happy to fully explain/disclose this project and intervention to a participant?
- Would you be confident that participants will not regret the decisions they've made, due to this intervention?
- Would you be proud of your work, if this intervention was published on the front page of a national newspaper?

Behavioral science also teaches us that salience is critical in instilling new habits and positive behaviors. Therefore, it's important to develop reminder systems for integrating behavioral science into daily activities. For example, we recently helped a financial services client to build "BeSci Checklists" into training and support materials for their advisors, as visible reminders to guide their client interactions. We've also built in "Ethical Implications" as a formal criterion upon which to screen and optimize proposed interventions ("nudges") prior to their implementation. Building these steps into the process, at both the project selection and executional level, serves to keep ethical considerations salient.

Applying Behavioral Science Ethically And Effectively

For business leaders, behavioral science represents both an opportunity and a responsibility. Clearly, there's the potential to drive profitable change, among both customers and employees. And inevitably, there's the temptation to jump immediately to opportunities and applications with the most immediate return and projected ROI.

However, it is wise to balance and guide these efforts with ethical considerations. By framing behavioral science properly, learning through Internal initiatives, finding the right projects and integrating ethical considerations within processes and reminder systems, leaders can lay the groundwork for lasting impact and success. Collectively, these steps will:

- Help promote internal acceptance and application
- Focus energies on efforts that are most likely to be successful, profitable and ethical
- Address and help mitigate concerns, by associating behavioral science with positive, pro-social change, rather than manipulation.

As importantly, they will help position behavioral science as a catalyst for a more sustainable approach to business, which aims to serve the long-term needs of all stakeholders (and society). Therefore, beyond infusing these new tools within our organisations, our larger goal should be to instil a new mindset, committed to the vision of applying behavioral science ethically and effectively.

Author Bios

Matthew Battersby

Matt Battersby is Chief Behavioral Scientist at the Reinsurance Group of America (RGA) where he focuses on applying behavioral science to issues of health and financial wellbeing. Matt was previously Managing Director and head of the behavioral science team at Hill + Knowlton Strategies. Matt has a Master of Science (MSc) in Behavioural Science from the London School of Economics and a Bachelor of Science (BSc) in Economics and Philosophy from the University of Bristol.

Chapter: The Centralized Team Approach

Kristen Berman

Kristen Berman is co-founder and CEO of Irrational Labs. Irrational Labs is a leading Silicon Valley behavioral research and design consultancy, working with the world's most influential businesses and institutions.

Chapter: Product Management

Charlotte Blank

As chief behavioral officer of Maritz, Charlotte Blank leads the incentive firm's psychological expertise in designing effective sales channel and employee performance programs.

Ever-curious about "what makes us work," Charlotte forges the connection between academic theory and business application by championing field experimentation as a means to unleash workforce potential.

Chapter: Why Organizations Use Behavioral Science

Linnea Gandhi

Linnea Gandhi teaches, researches, and consults on how to integrate behavioral theories and experimentation into business settings. She founded BehavioralSight to help professionals become better architects of their employees', their customers', and their own behaviors. Also affiliated with both Chicago Booth and Wharton, Linnea is currently working on two problem areas: (1) building a phenotype of effective nudges and (2) improving our ability to learn from error.

Chapter: The Integrated Model

Nicole Grabel

Nicole Grabel is a Principal of Behavioral Science at BehavioralSight. Previously working in brand strategy, she now helps clients apply behavioral science principles to help them make more informed decisions when it comes to their consumers, their organizations, and themselves.

Chapter: Improving Strategic Decisions

Erik Johnson

Erik Johnson is the founder of Behavioral Strategies LLC, where he uses behavioral methods to help organizations improve product and marketing performance and enhance organizational decision-making capabilities. Previously, he co-created ProductPsychology.com and held roles at ideas42 and Morningstar.

Chapter: Marketing

Meghann Johnson

Meghann Johnson is a Principal of Behavioral Science at BehavioralSight and the Director of Behavioral Intervention Design and User Experience at the Texas Behavioral Science and Policy Institute. She gets excited about using behavioral science to inform decision processes and testing through experimentation, both in RCTs and to applied business problems in the field.

Chapter: Improving Strategic Decisions

Zarak Khan

Zarak Khan is a behavioral scientist with experience generating and applying insights to organizational strategy, innovation infrastructure, product design, public policy, process improvement, and program management. He is a Senior Behavioral Researcher at the Center for Advanced Hindsight, a Behavioral Science Fellow at the University of Pennsylvania, and a board member of Action Design Network.

Chapters: Preface, The Current State Of Behavioral Teams, Innovation, Consulting

Rachelle Martino

Rachelle is a partner at BehavioralSight. Years of experience in management consulting and industry has left a deep appreciation and passion for the challenges and opportunities that await those who seek to employ behavioral science in the business setting. She enjoys seeing ideas brought to life through application and real-world pressure testing.

Chapter: Research in the Real World

Laurel Newman

Laurel Newman is a behavioral scientist at Edward Jones. A former college professor, she now works with teams throughout the organization to improve the experiences of clients and employees by applying behavioral science principles and testing their impact.

Chapters: Preface, The Current State Of Behavioral Teams, Employee Culture and Human Resources, Team Structure Intro

Namika Sagara

Namika Sagara is a Co-Founder and Chief Behavioral Officer at Syntoniq, where she leads R&D for Tech and also is building and leading the Consulting team. Prior to Syntoniq, Dr. Sagara was a Founder and President of the industry's first Behavioral Science Center at Ipsos. Before her time at Ipsos, she was a President of Sagara Consulting, a postdoc and a visiting scholar at Duke University, and a research consultant at Center for Behavioral Finance at Allianz Global Investors.

Chapter: Consumer and Market Research

Greg Szwartz

Greg is the healthcare data science practice lead at Deloitte Consulting. He has over 25 years of experience putting models and algorithms into life sciences and healthcare workflow—either strategic decisions around product development or capacity planning, or in operational workflow related to care management and patient support.

Chapter: Data Science and Measurement

Steve Wendel

Dr. Wendel is the head of Behavioral Science at Morningstar, where his team develops and tests practical techniques to help people overcome common behavioral obstacles in their finances. Steve is the author of three books on applied behavioral science and founder of the non-profit Action Design Network. He has two wonderful kids and a wife who don't care about behavioral science at all.

Chapter: The Current State of Behavioral Teams

Scott Young

Scott Young is a Senior Vice President of the BVA Group. He assumed this role after 20 years leading PRS (Perception Research Services) and later PRS IN VIVO, a Top-25 global shopper insights agency. Scott is passionate about finding "win-win-win" opportunities (that benefit companies, consumers and society)—and in applying behavioral science to help individuals and organizations make better decisions and adopt healthier, more sustainable habits.

Chapter: Getting Started with an Ethical Foundation